The Adventures of Rangi

Volume Three

By Jeri McCutcheon

Coyote Creek Books | San José | California

ISBN-978-1-946647-17-7

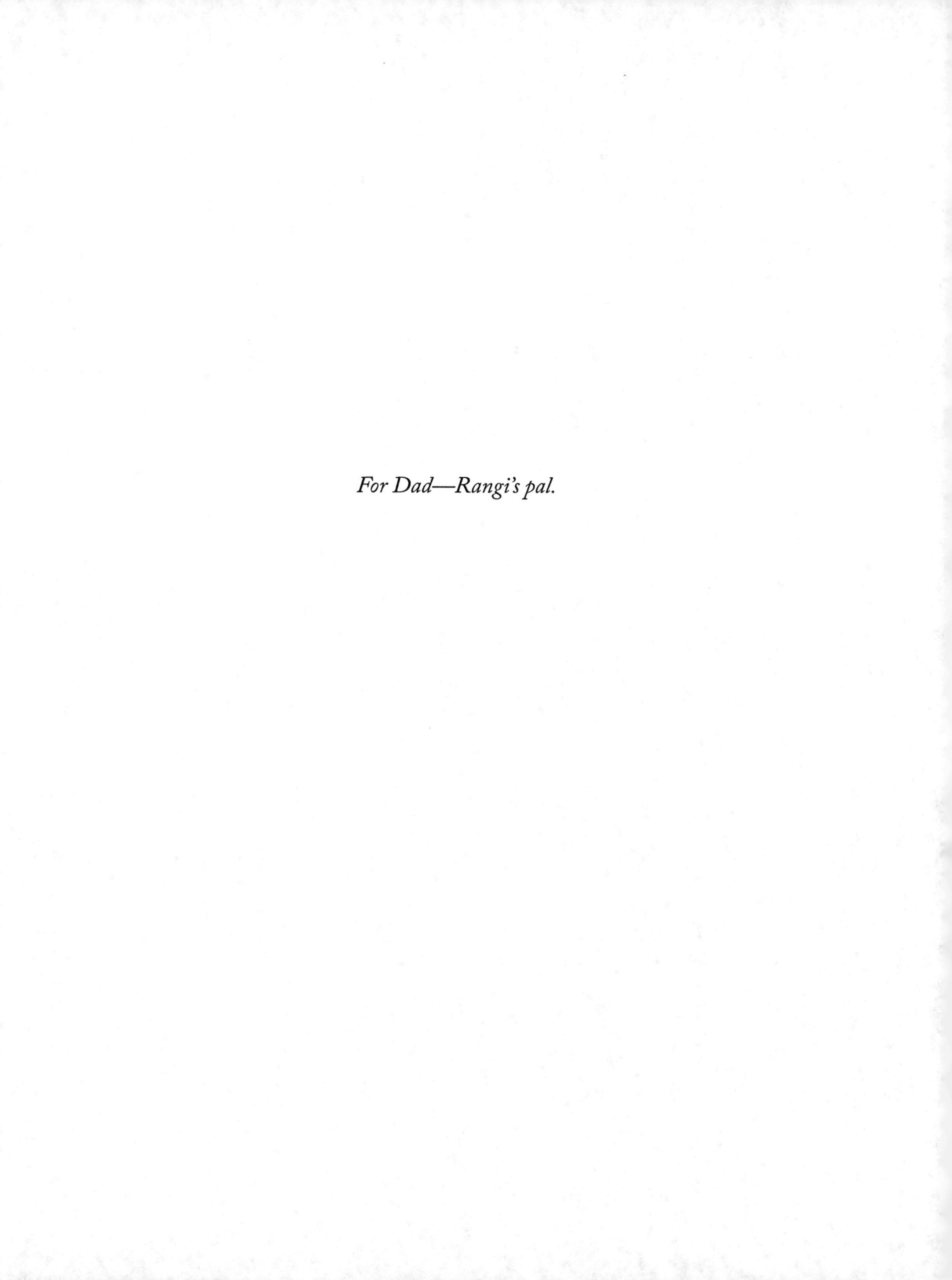

For Dad—Rangi's pal.

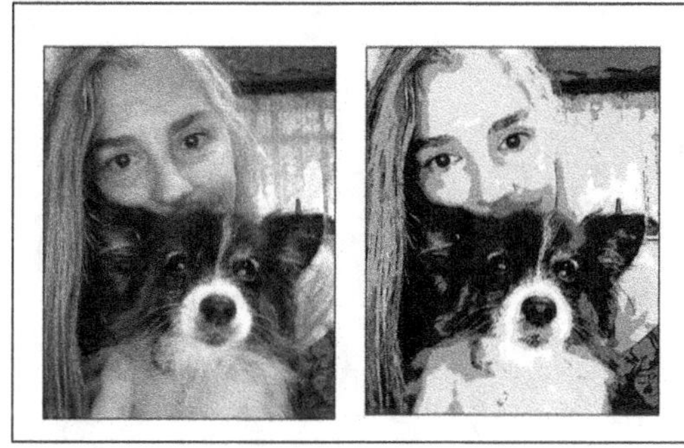

Artist **Jeri McCutcheon** is the third daughter, the twisted sister. When she's not drawing she's teaching tai chi or yoga. Still awaiting her chance to contort into a tiny box for the circus.

Rangi is celebrationing his 10th birthday with his pals in Adventures Near and Far. He's likes cuddling, doing yoga, playing with Josie girl next-door and walking back to the new farm and meeting the horses. Rangi is a papillon. The breed name means butterfly in French, based on the silhouette created by the long fringed hair on the ears.

Join us!
You can follow Jeri and Rangi on social media at: https://www.facebook.com/theadventuresofrangi and instagram #rangi_coloringbook.

Submit photos of your furry or feathered friend and they might be featured in future books.

RANGI'S SPOT

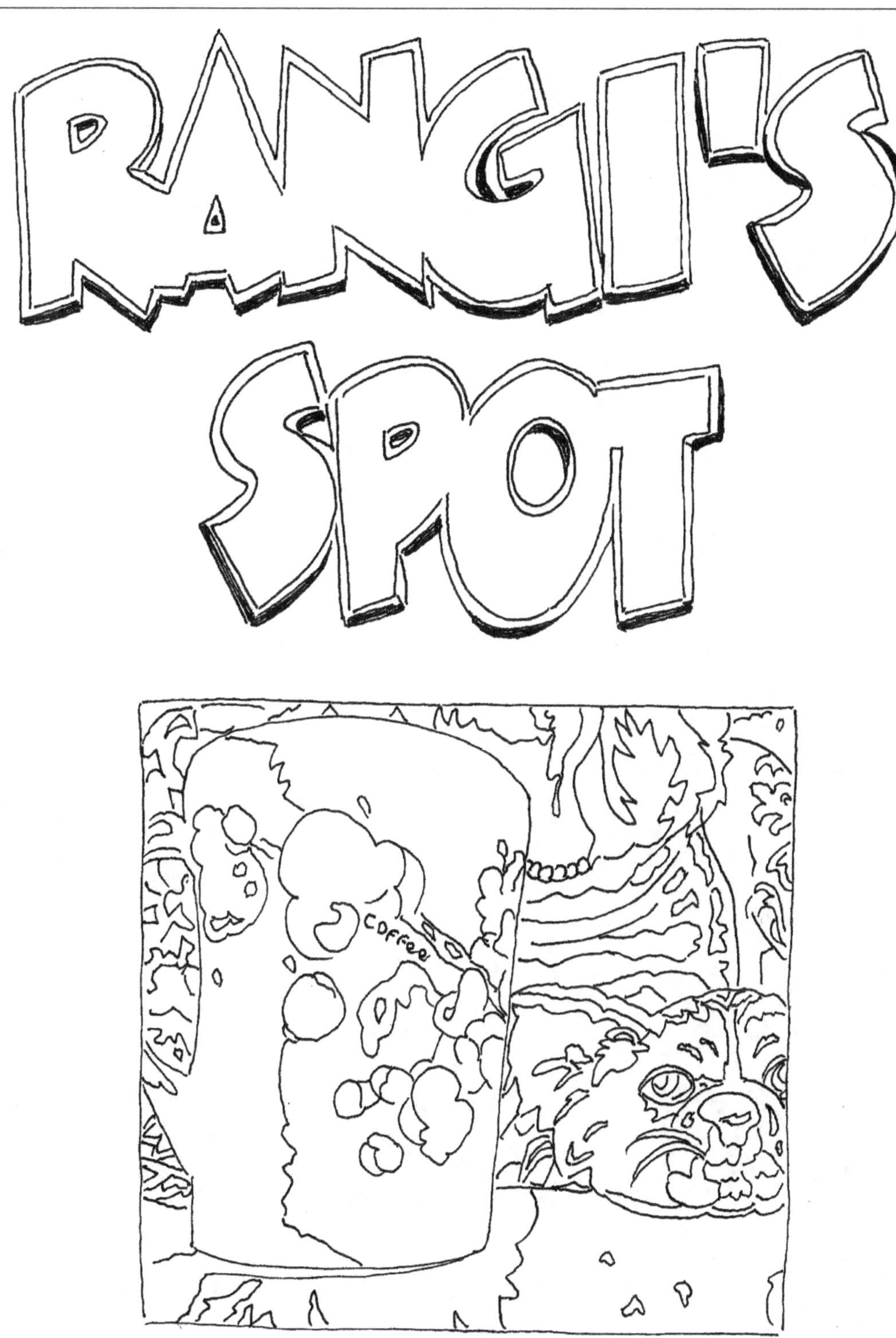

happy birthday Rangi

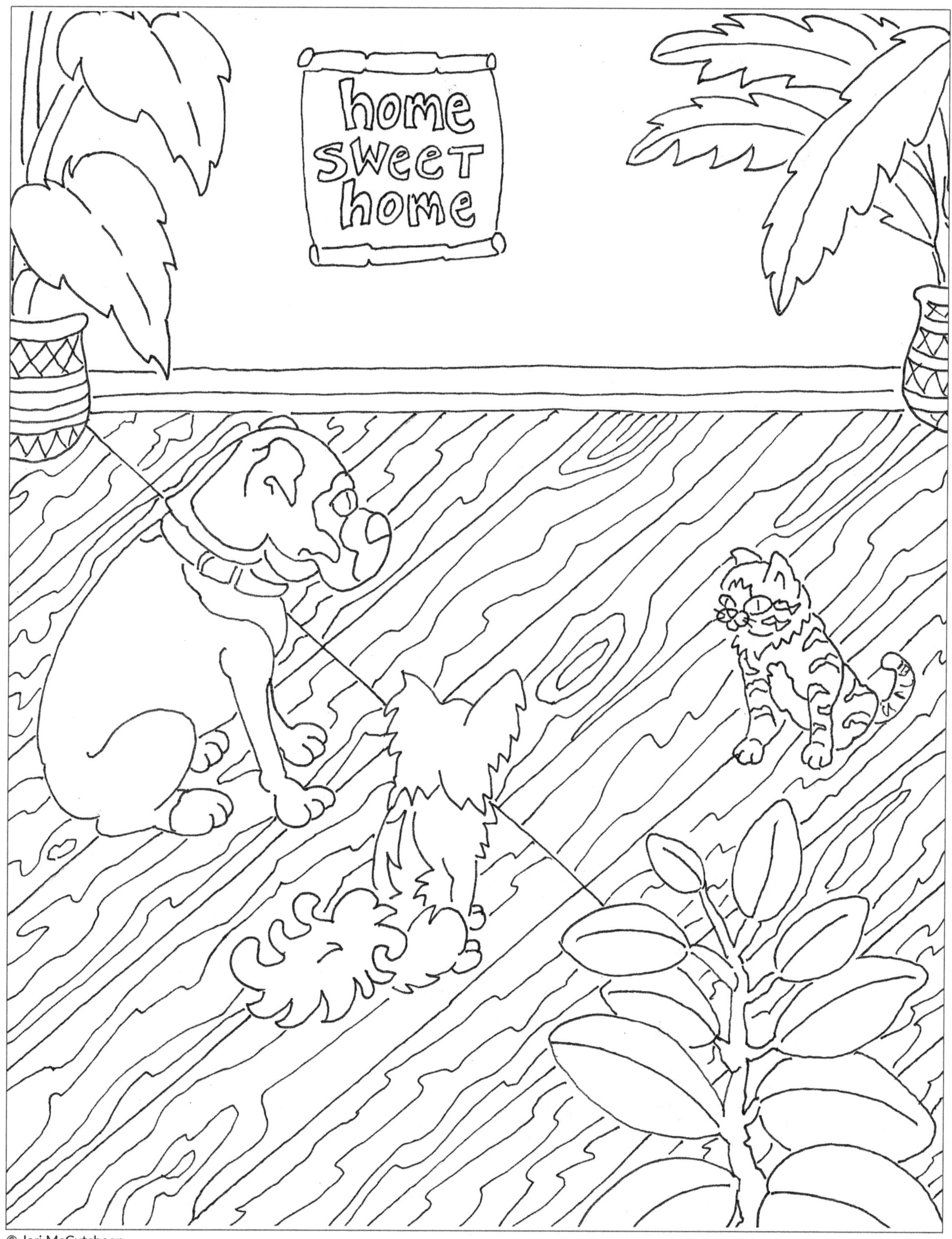

home
sweet
home

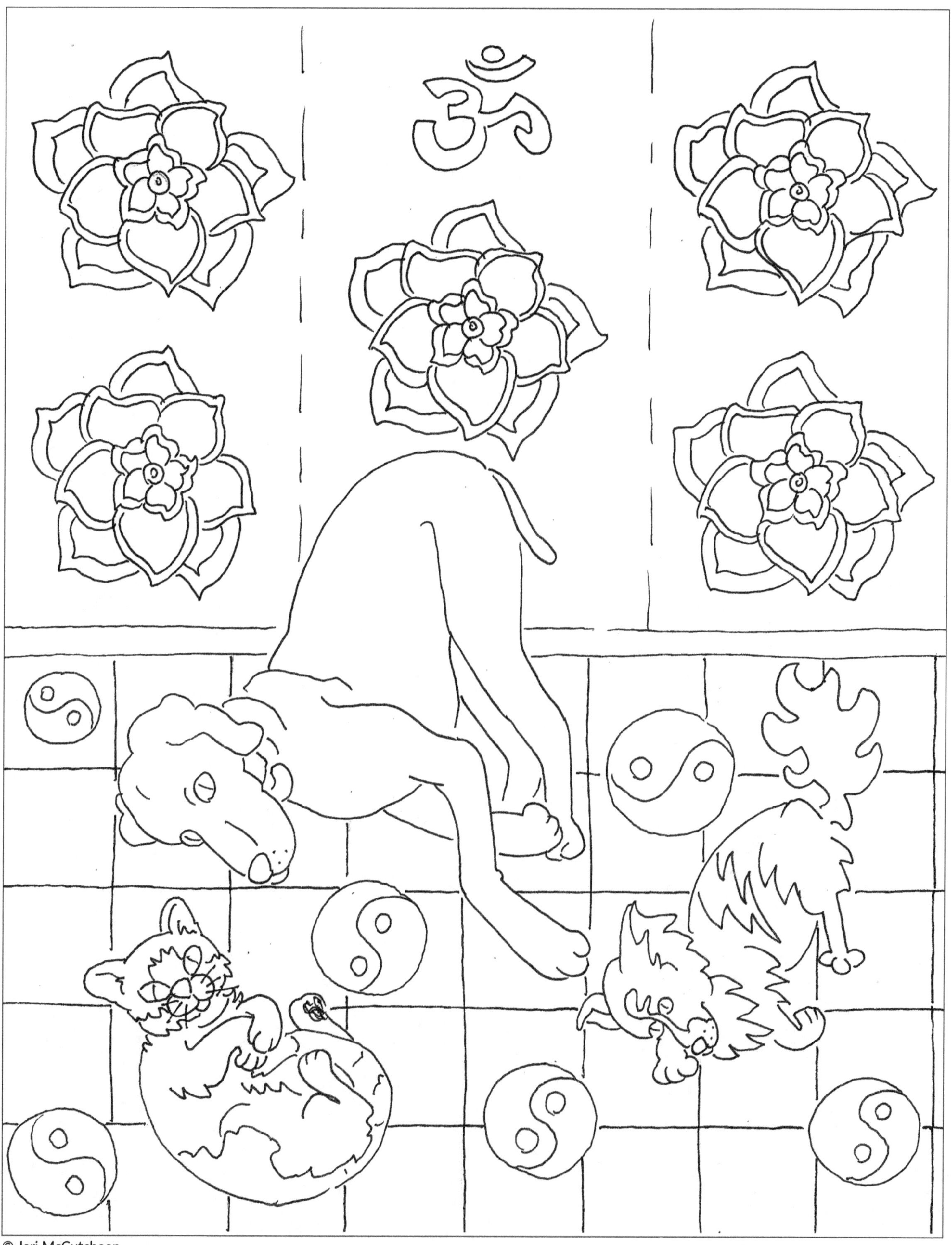

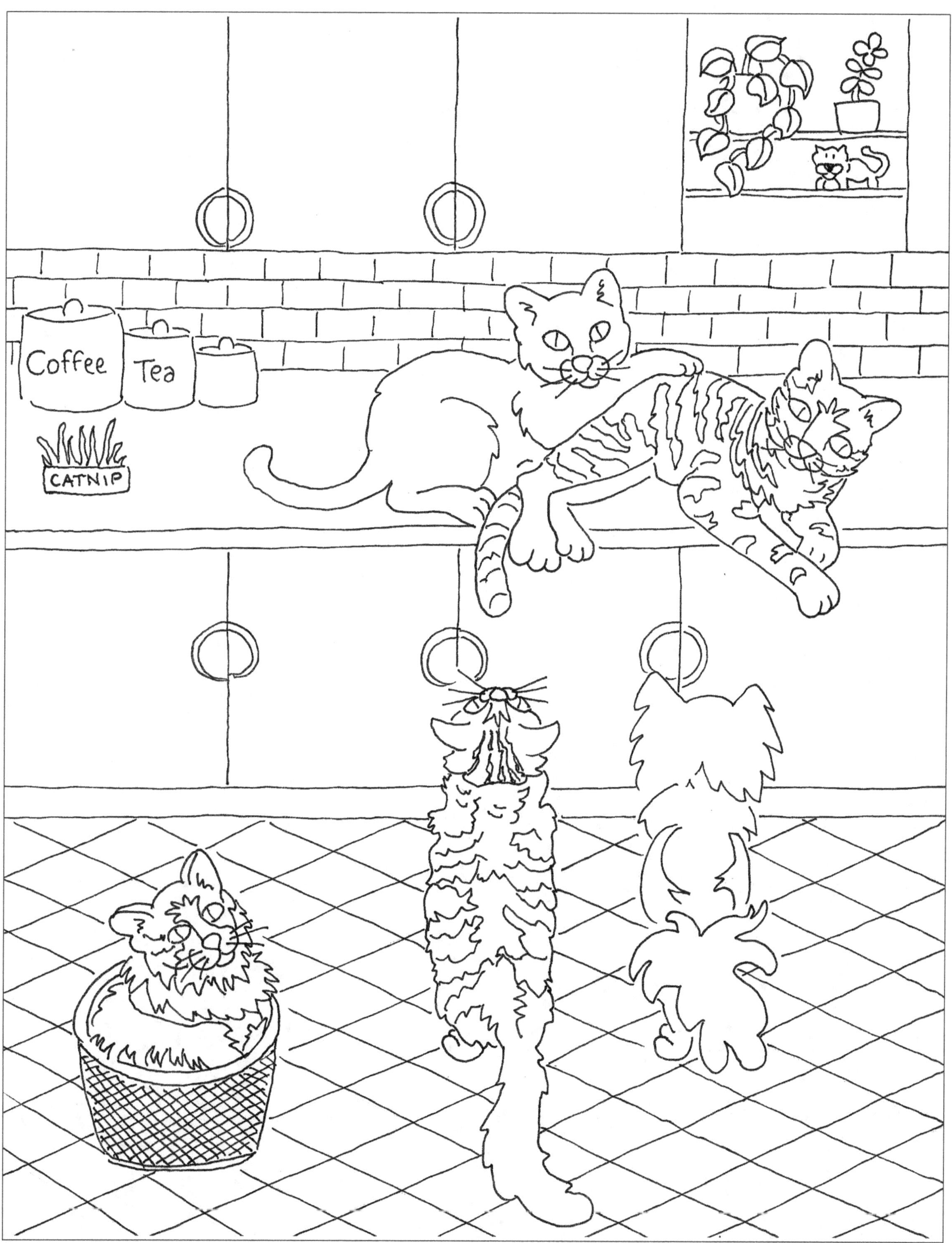

© Jeri McCutcheon

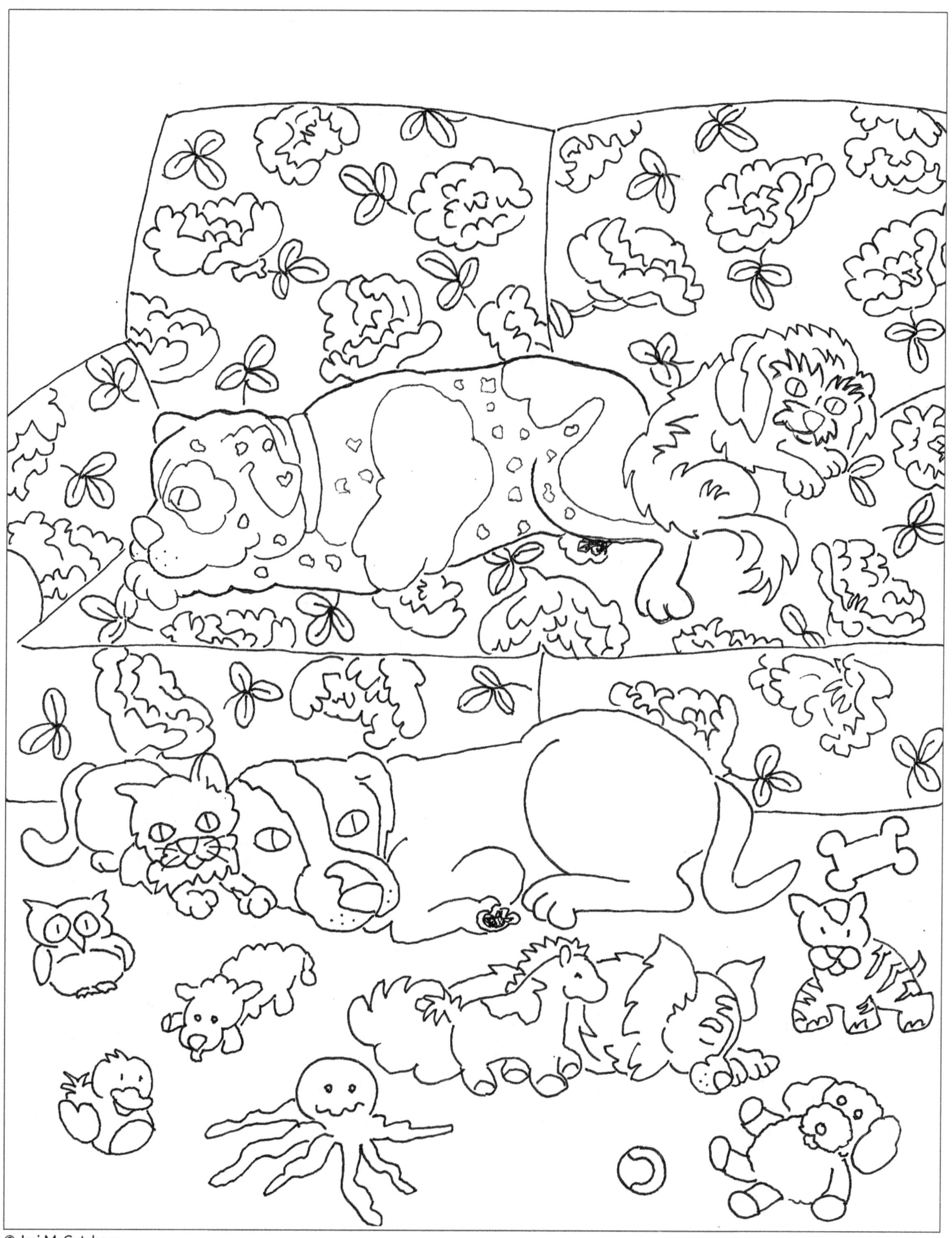

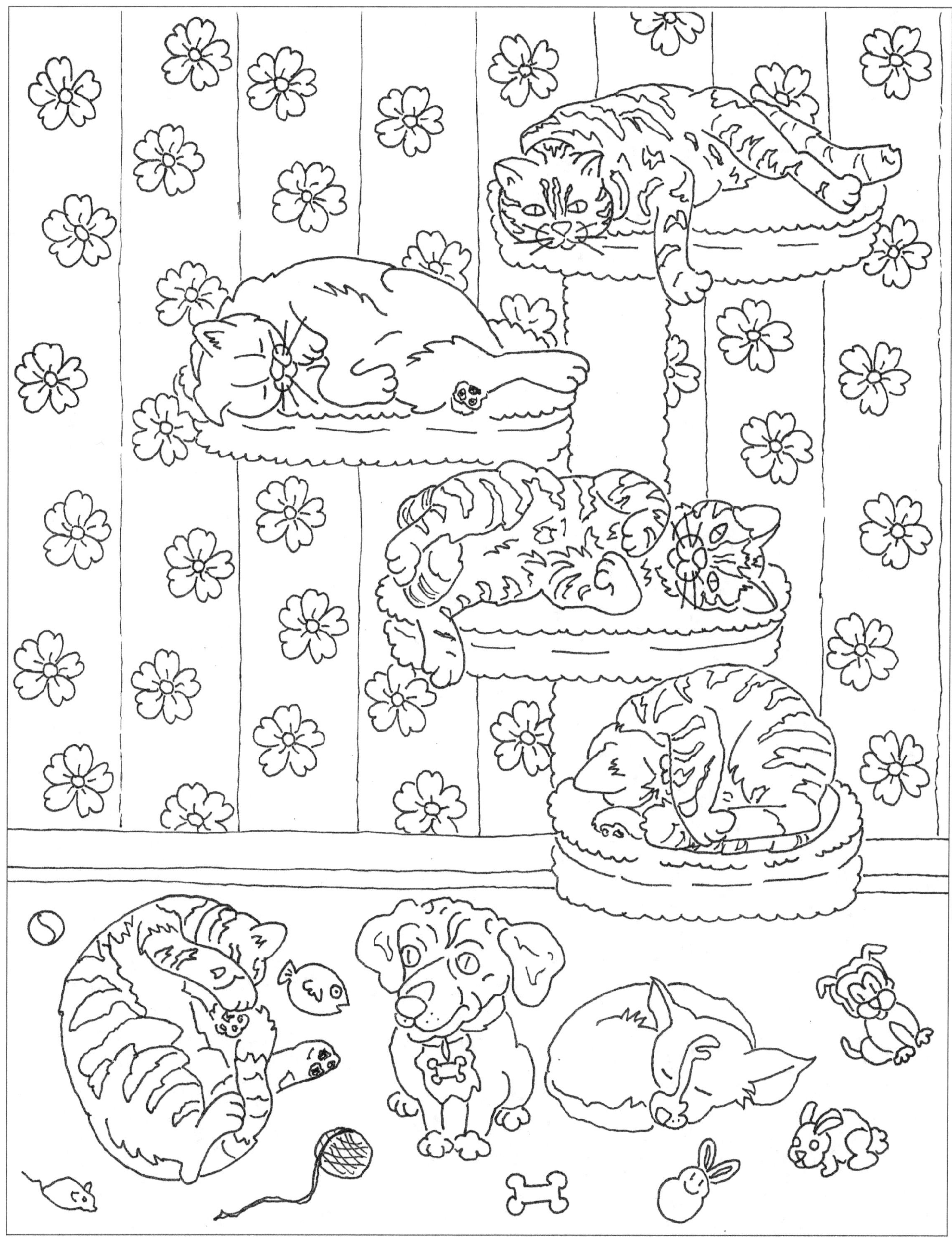

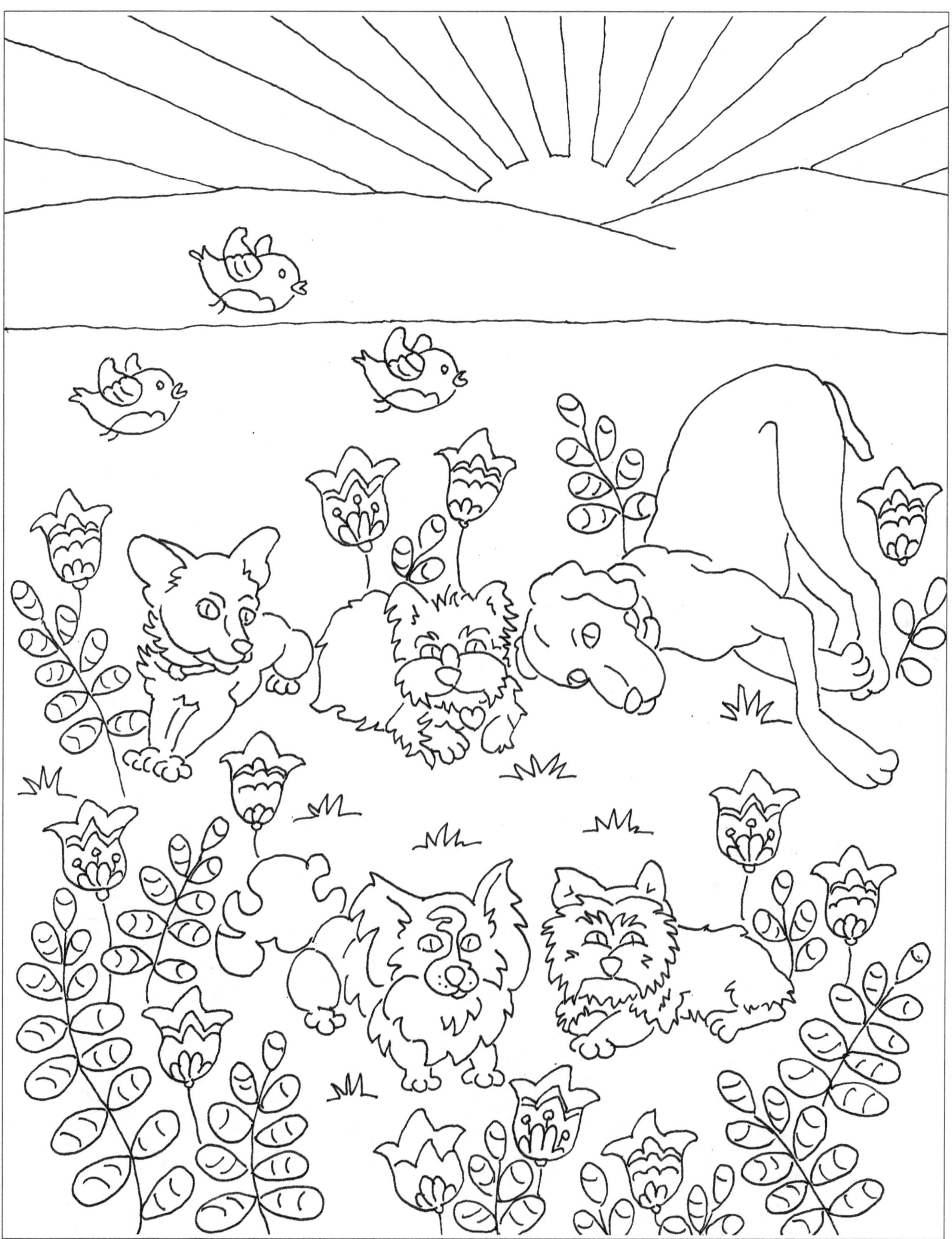

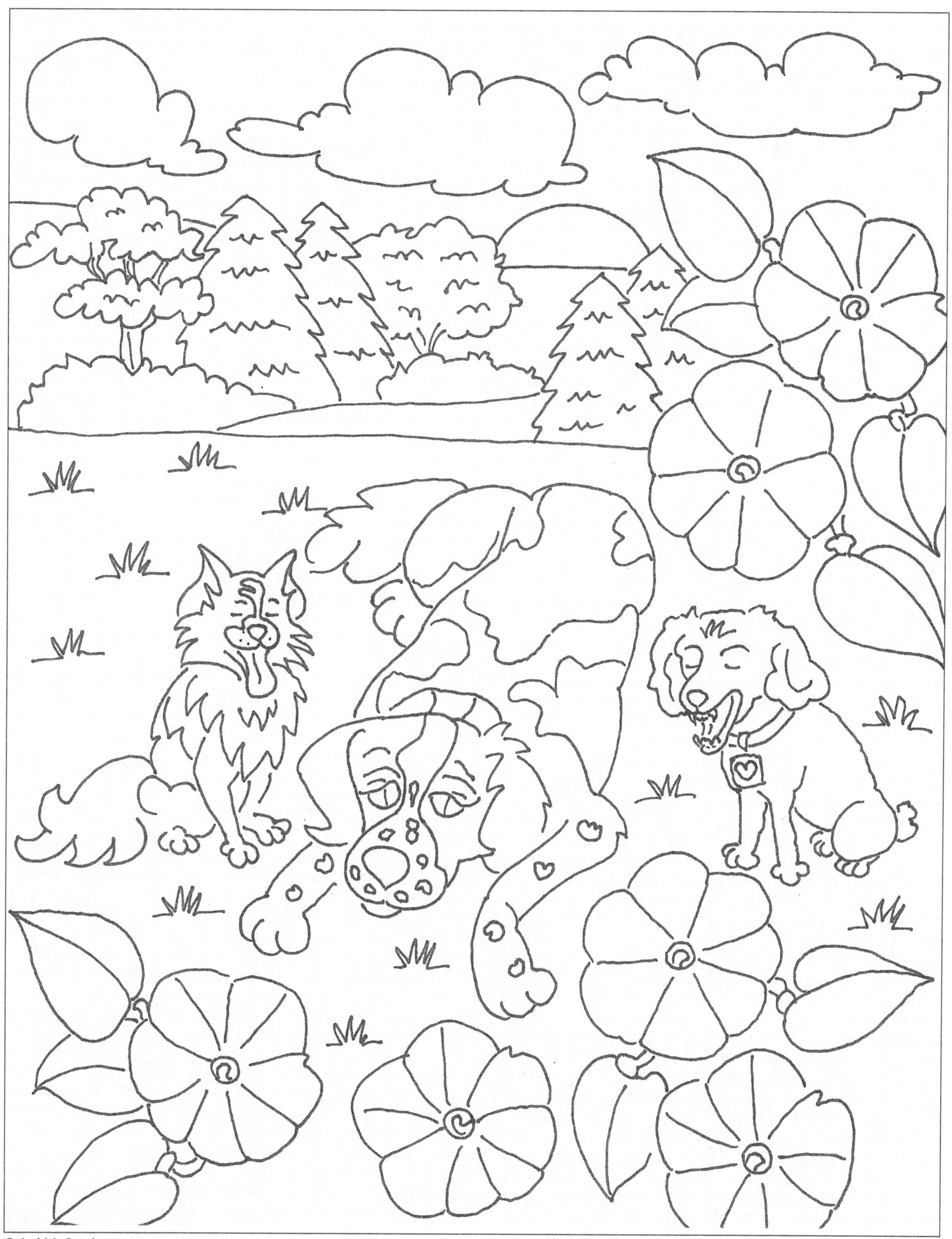

© Jeri McCutcheon

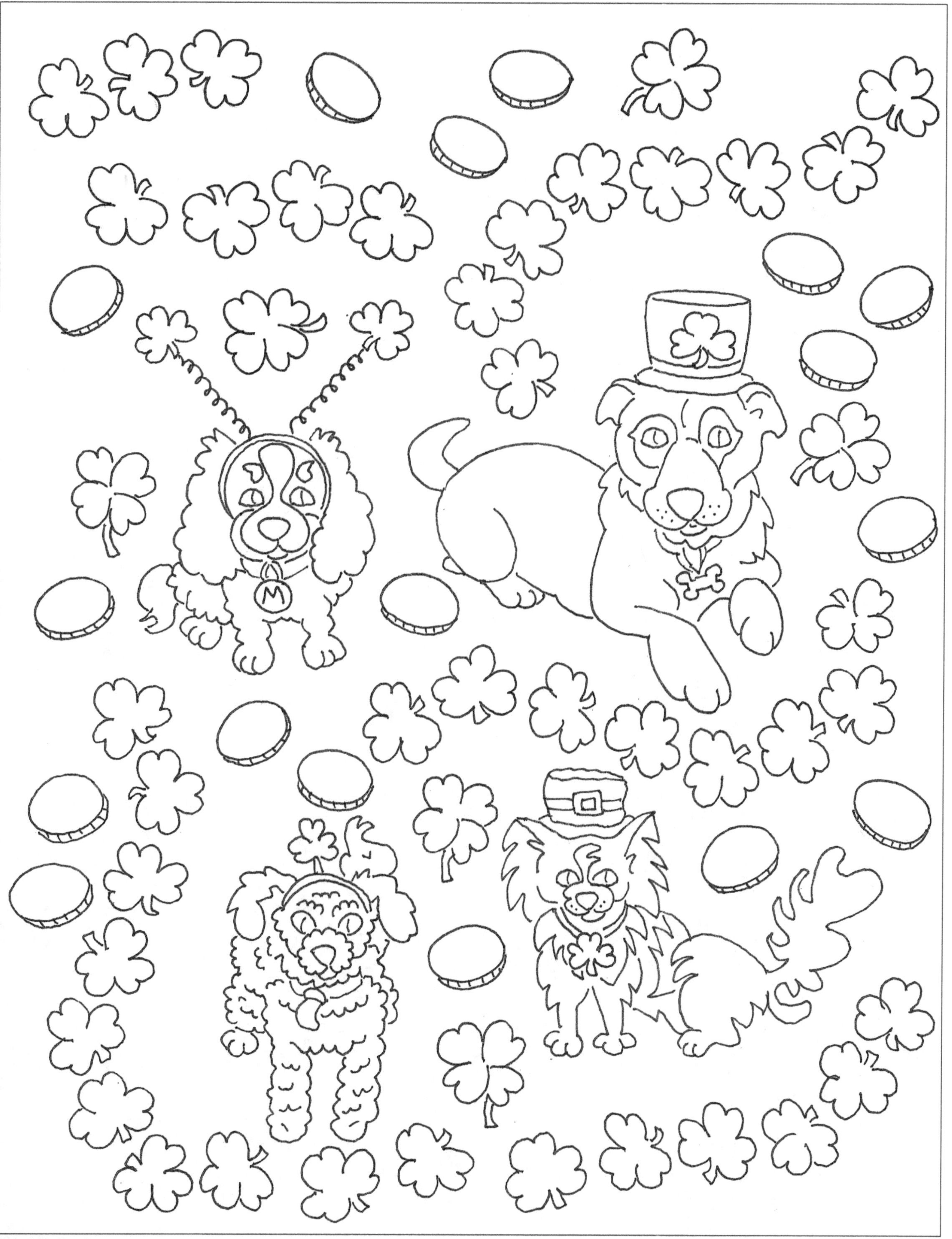

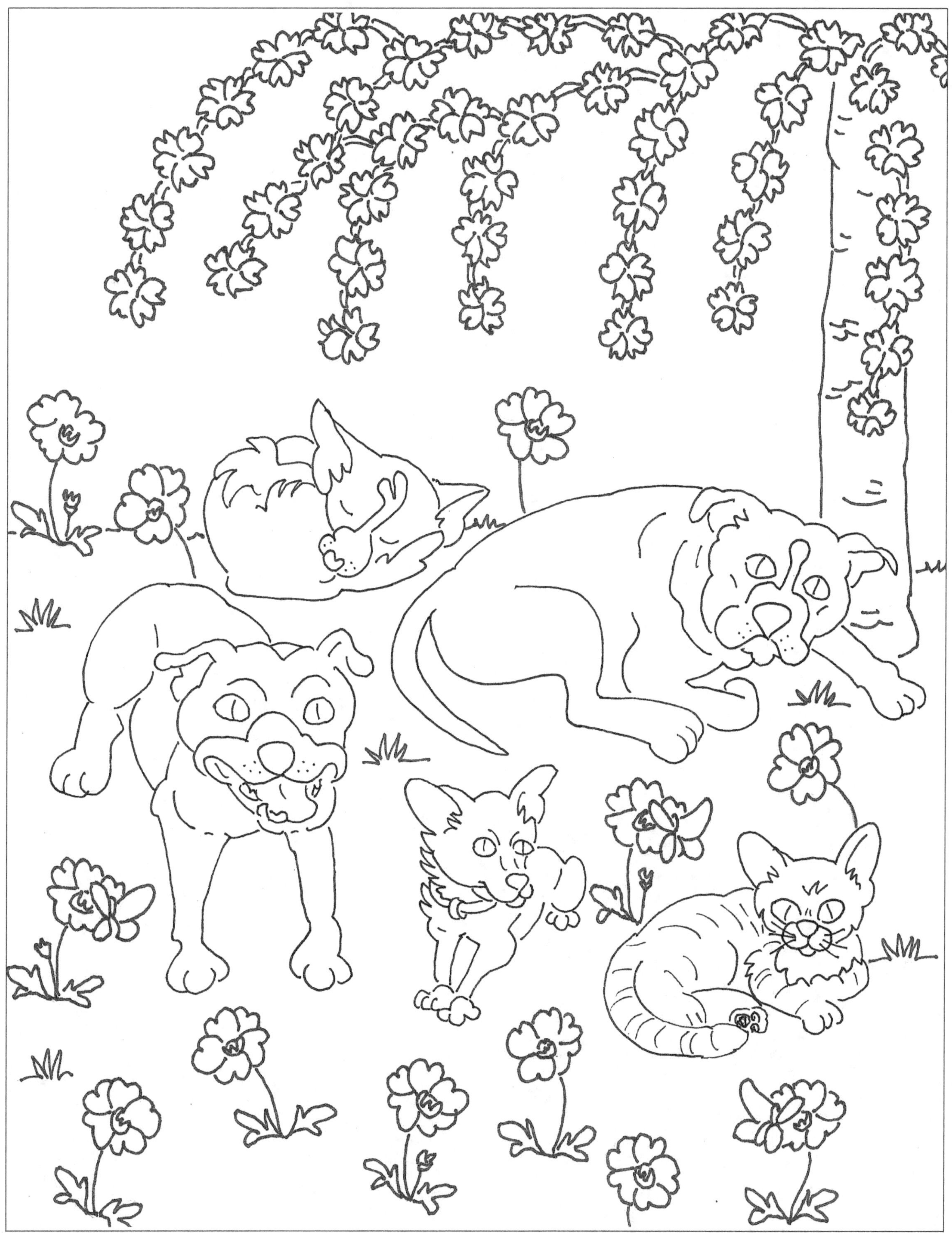

© Jeri McCutcheon

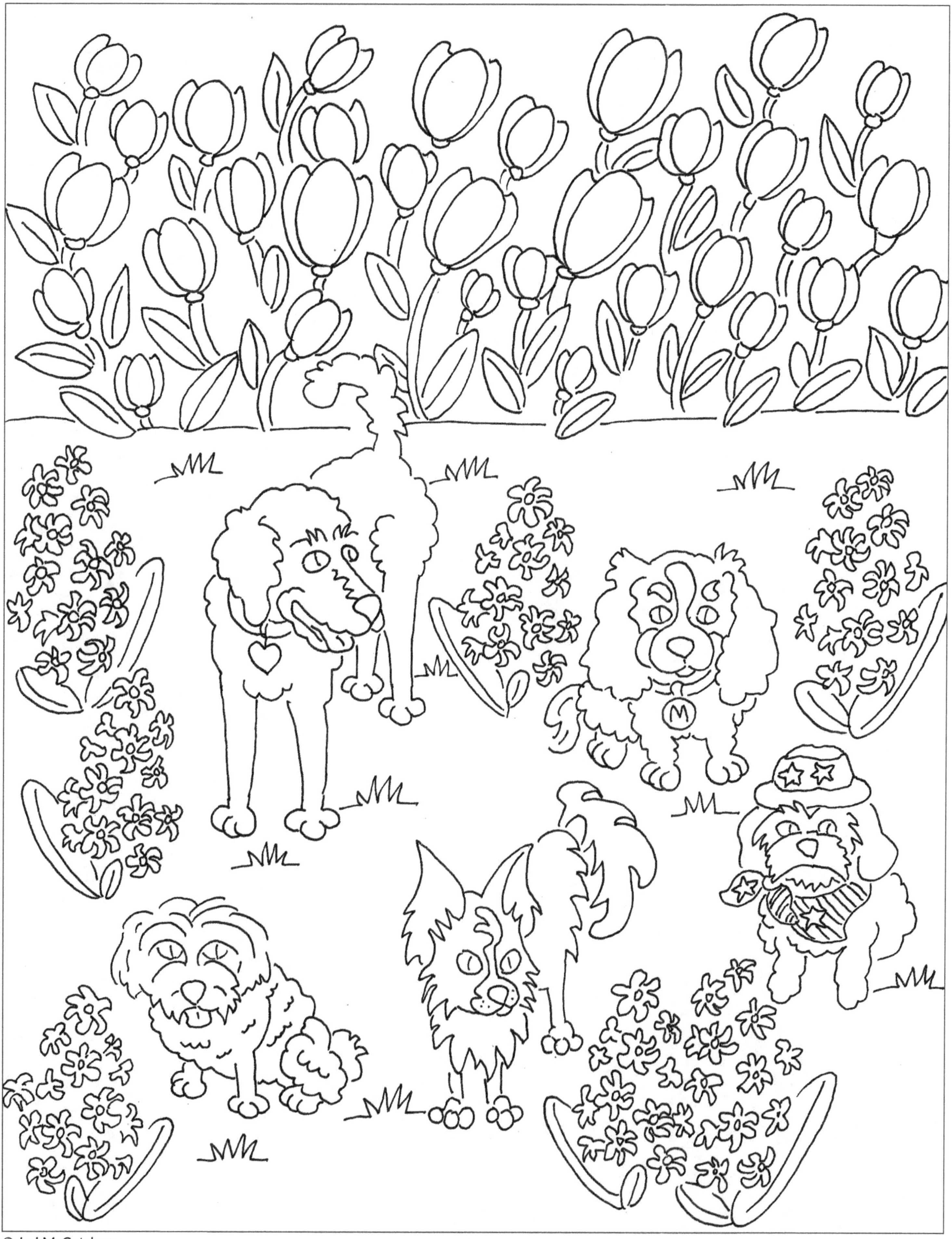

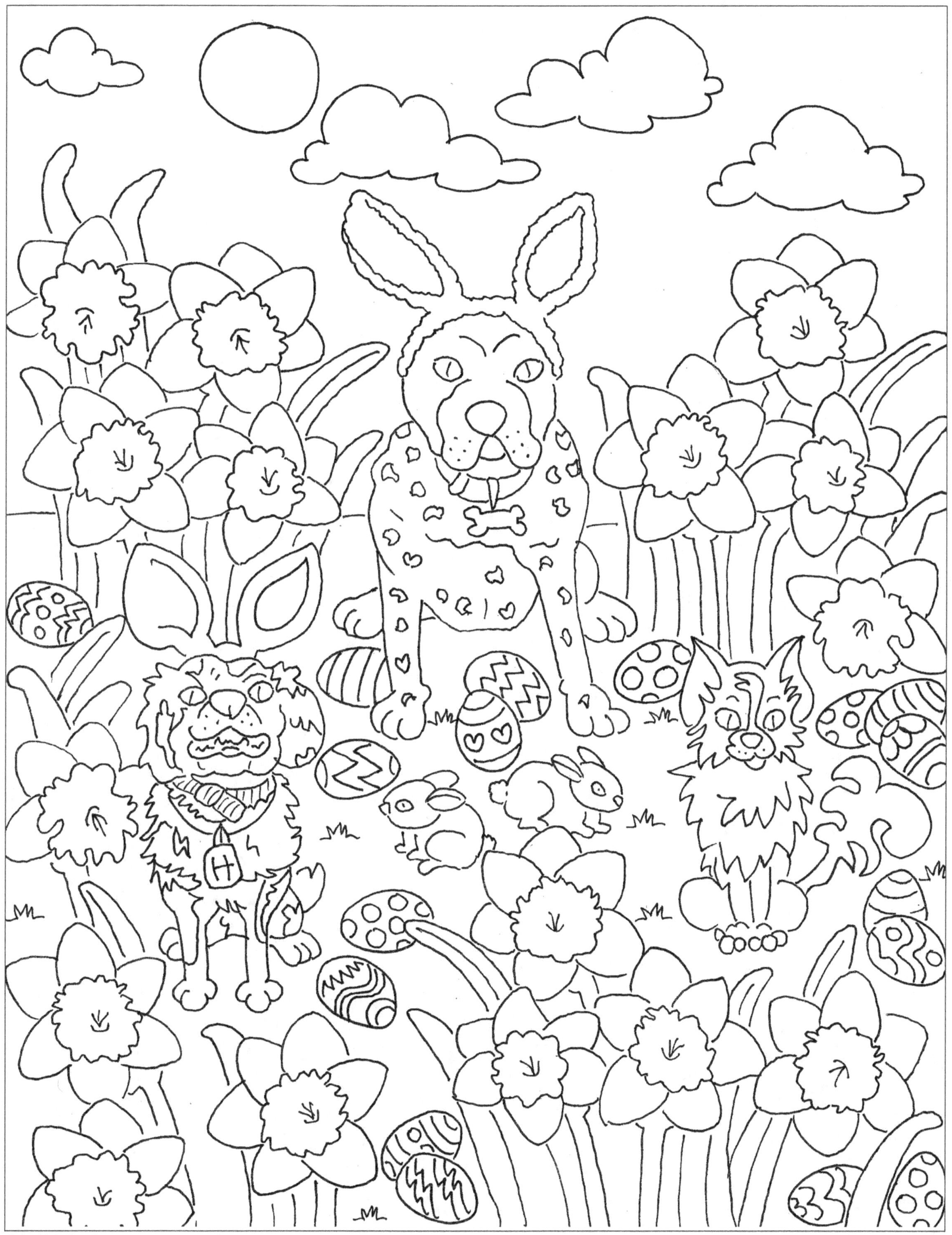

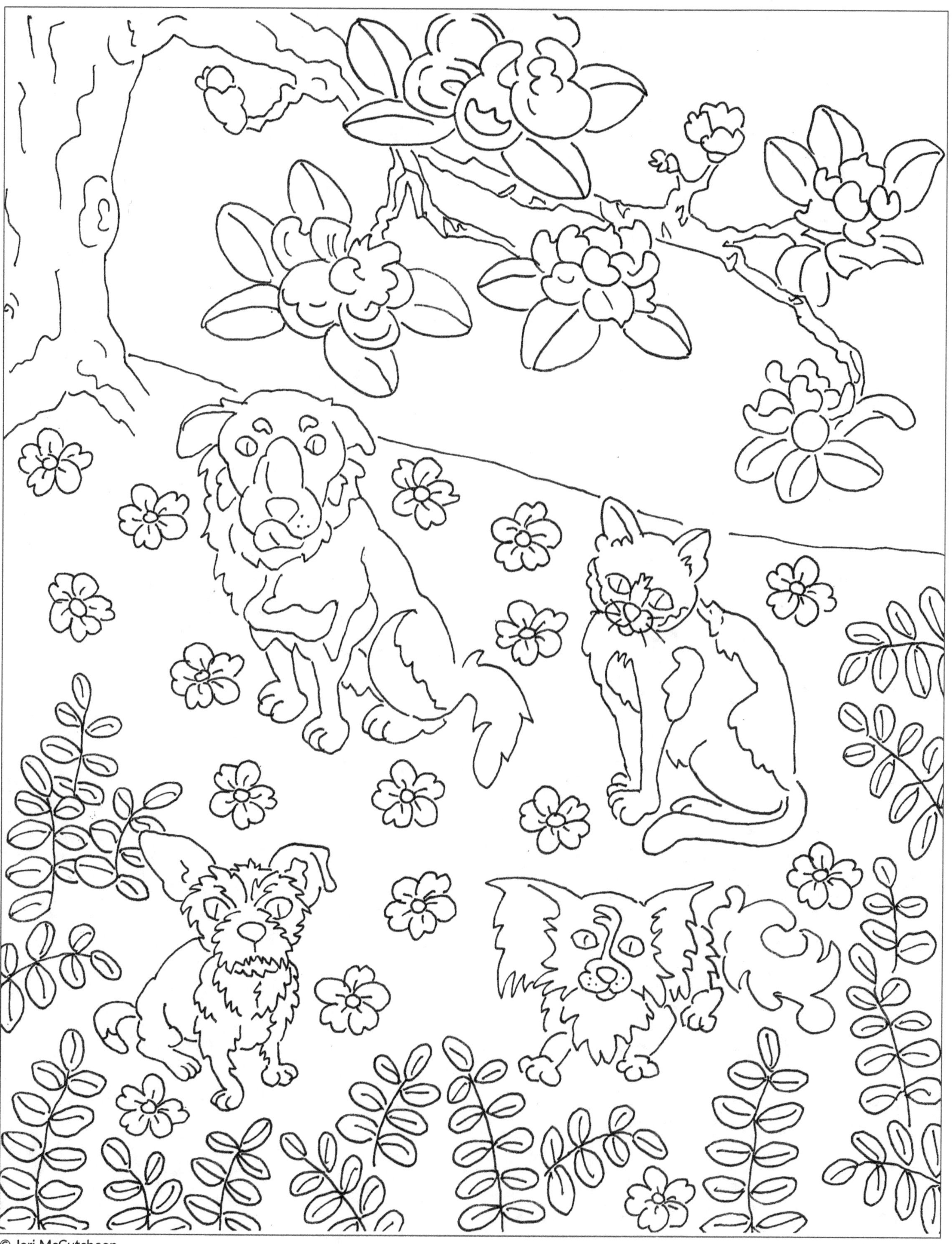

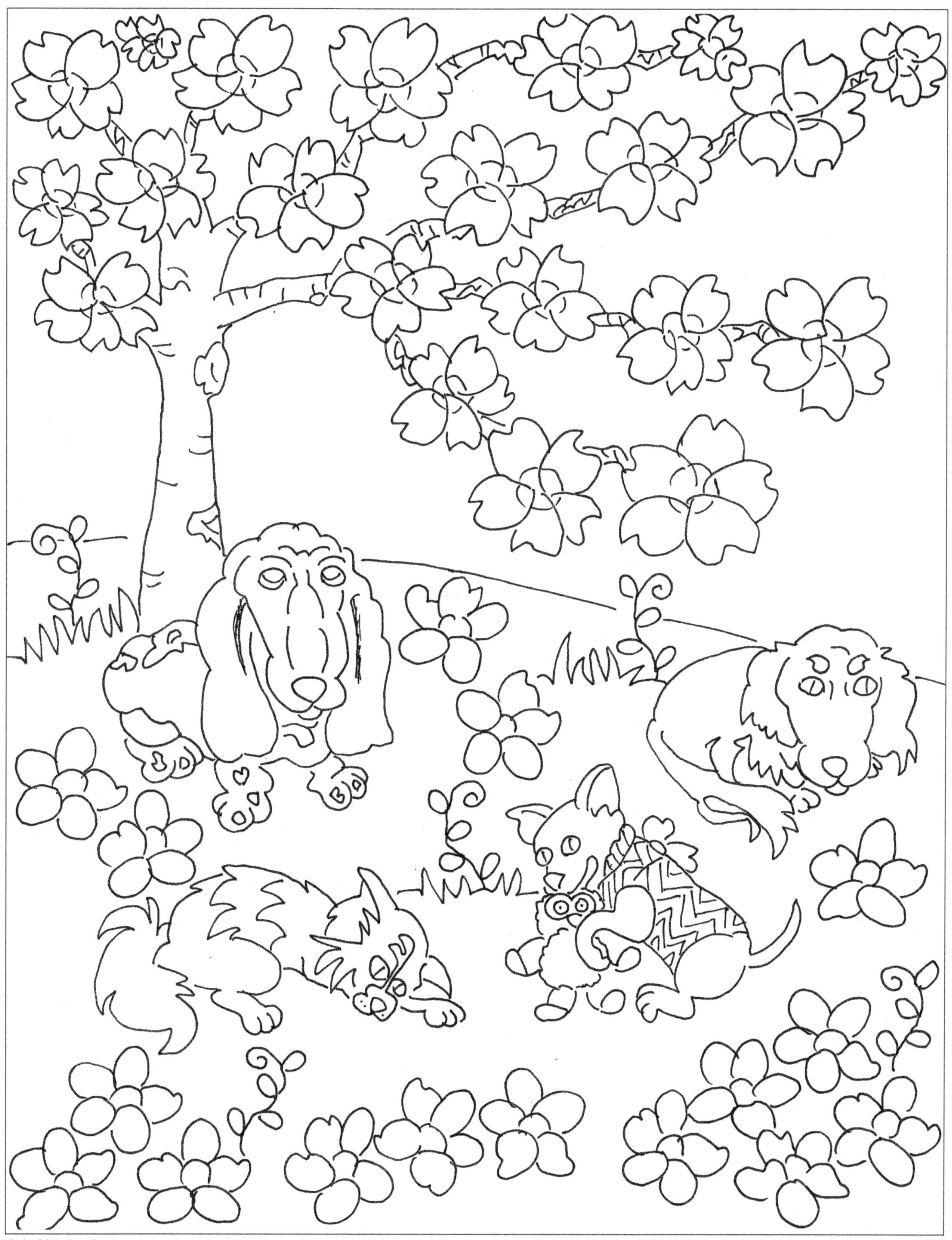

© Jeri McCutcheon

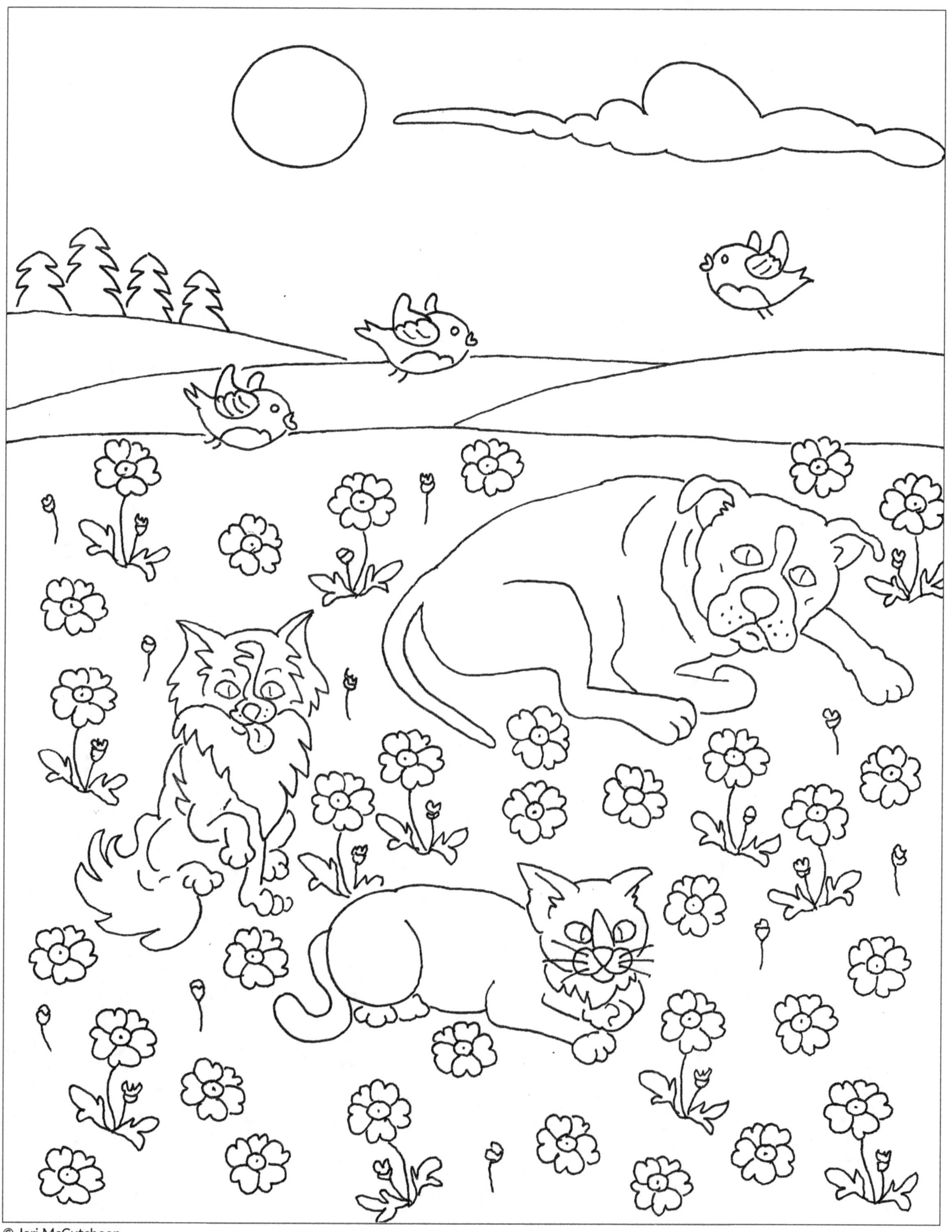

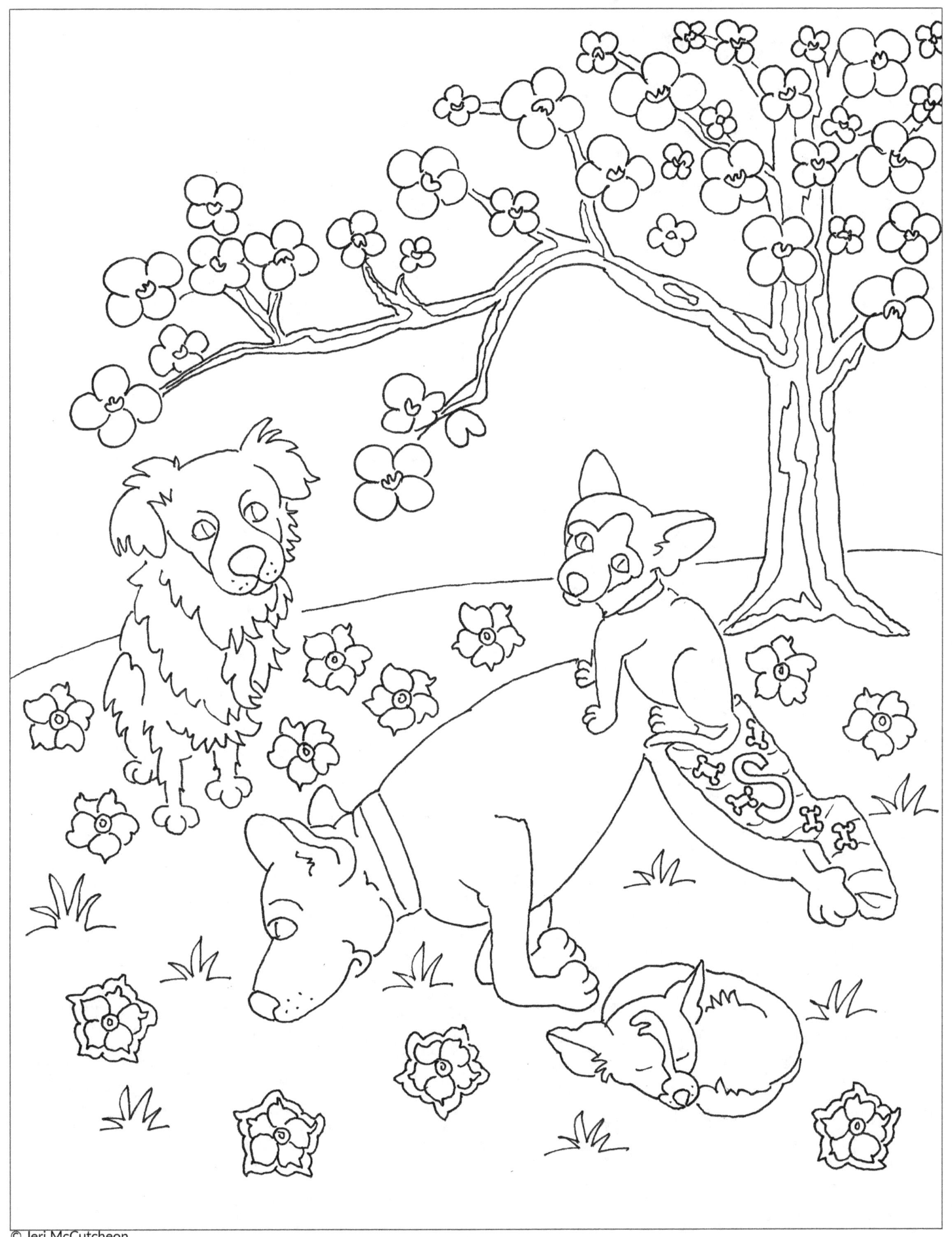

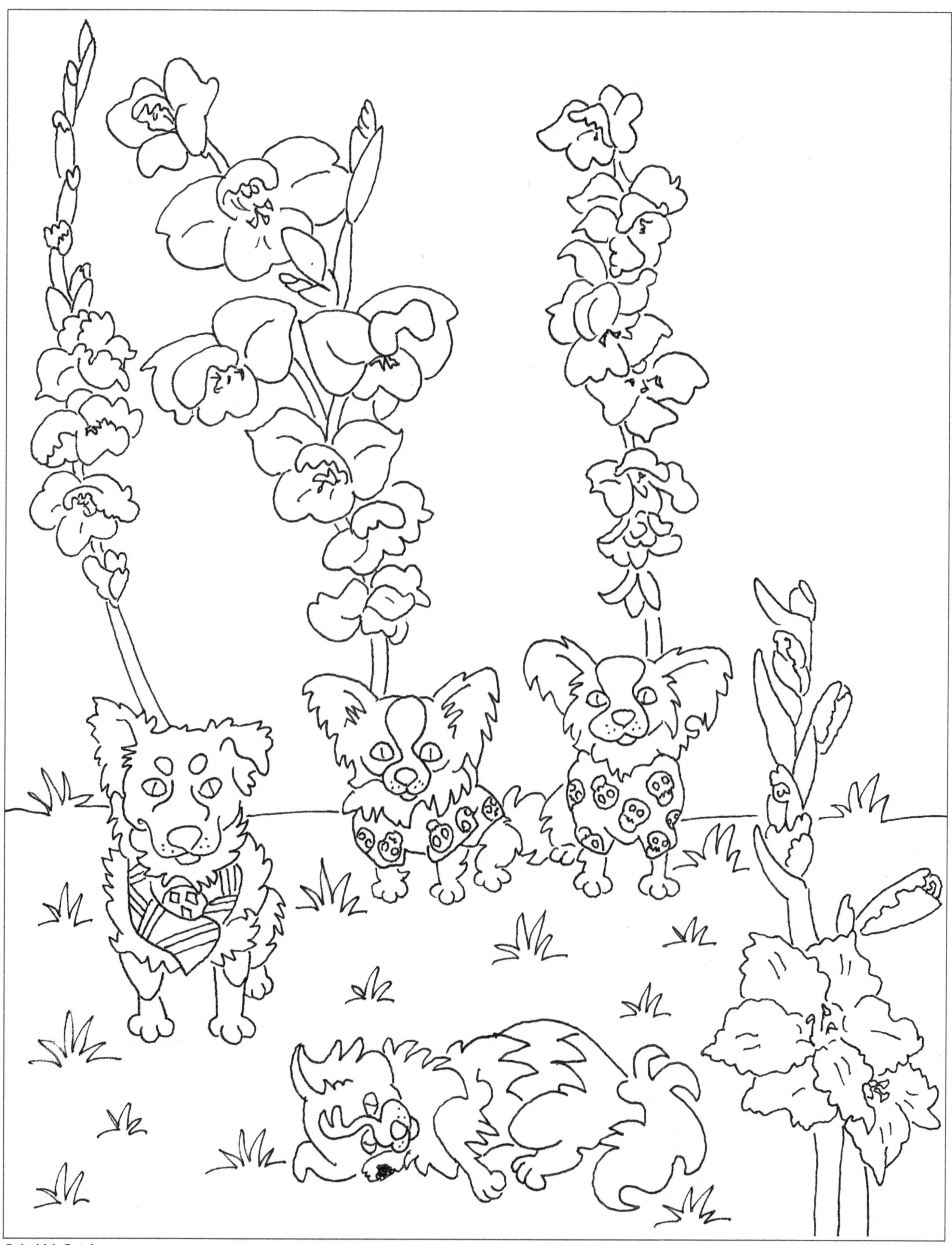

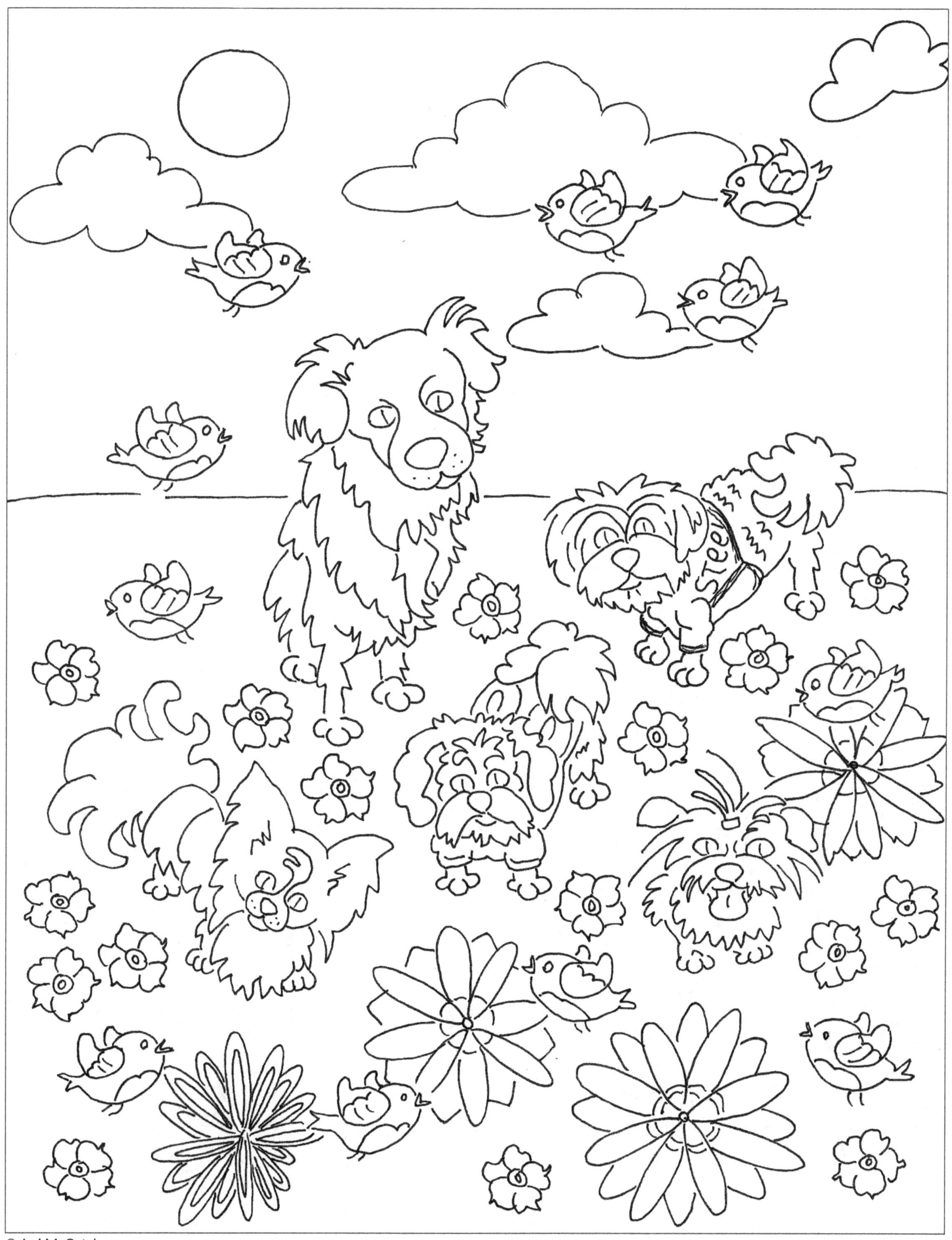

© Jeri McCutcheon

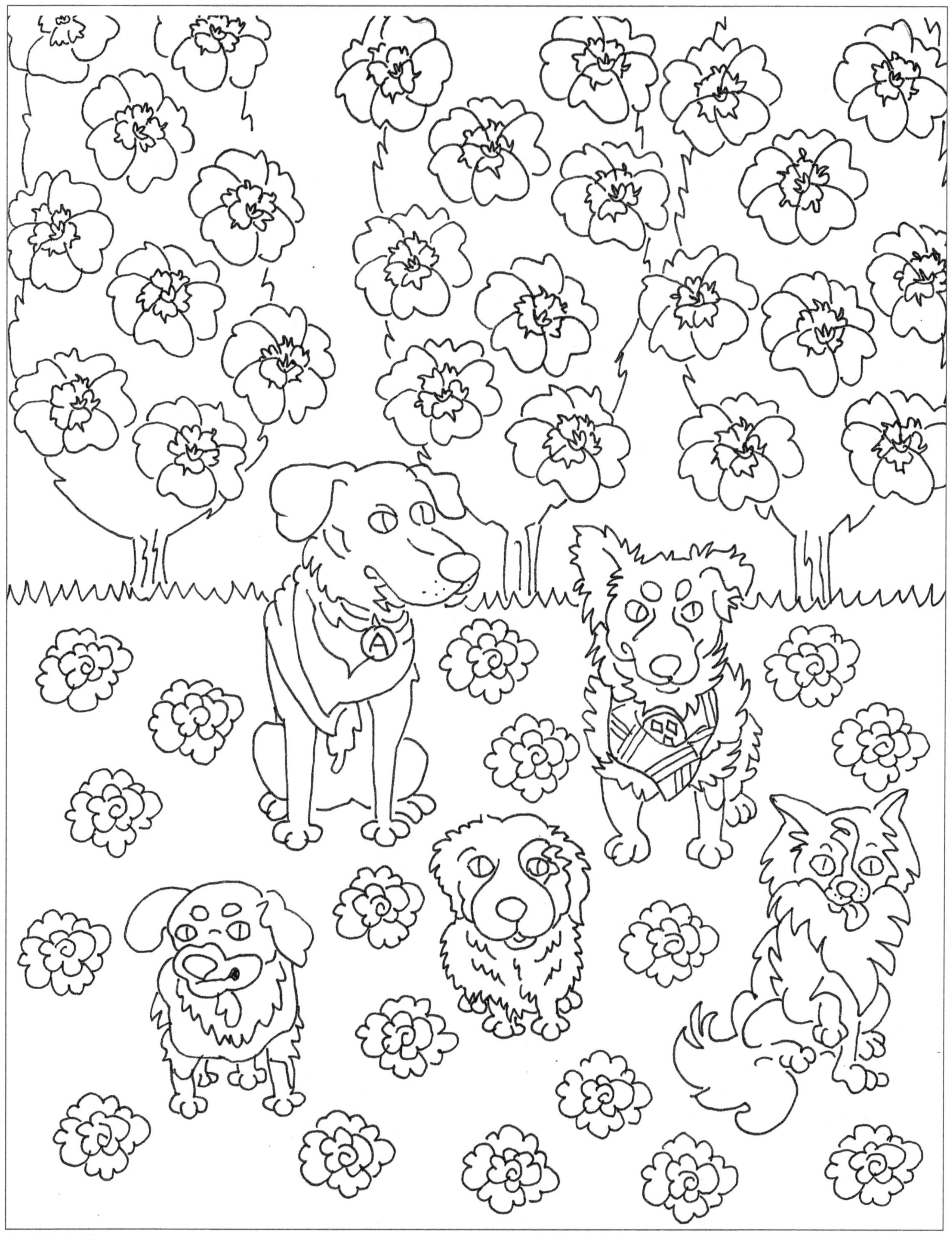

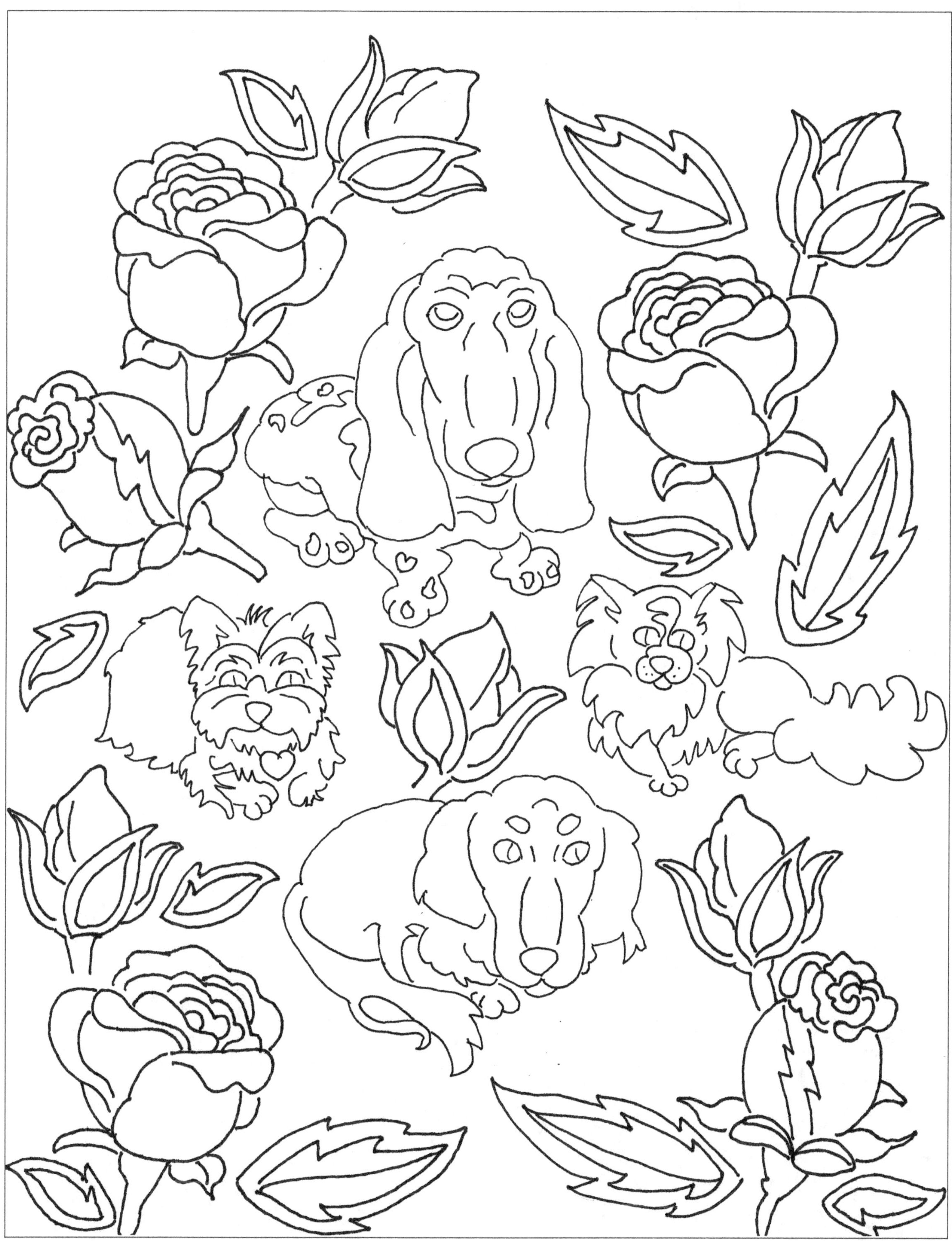

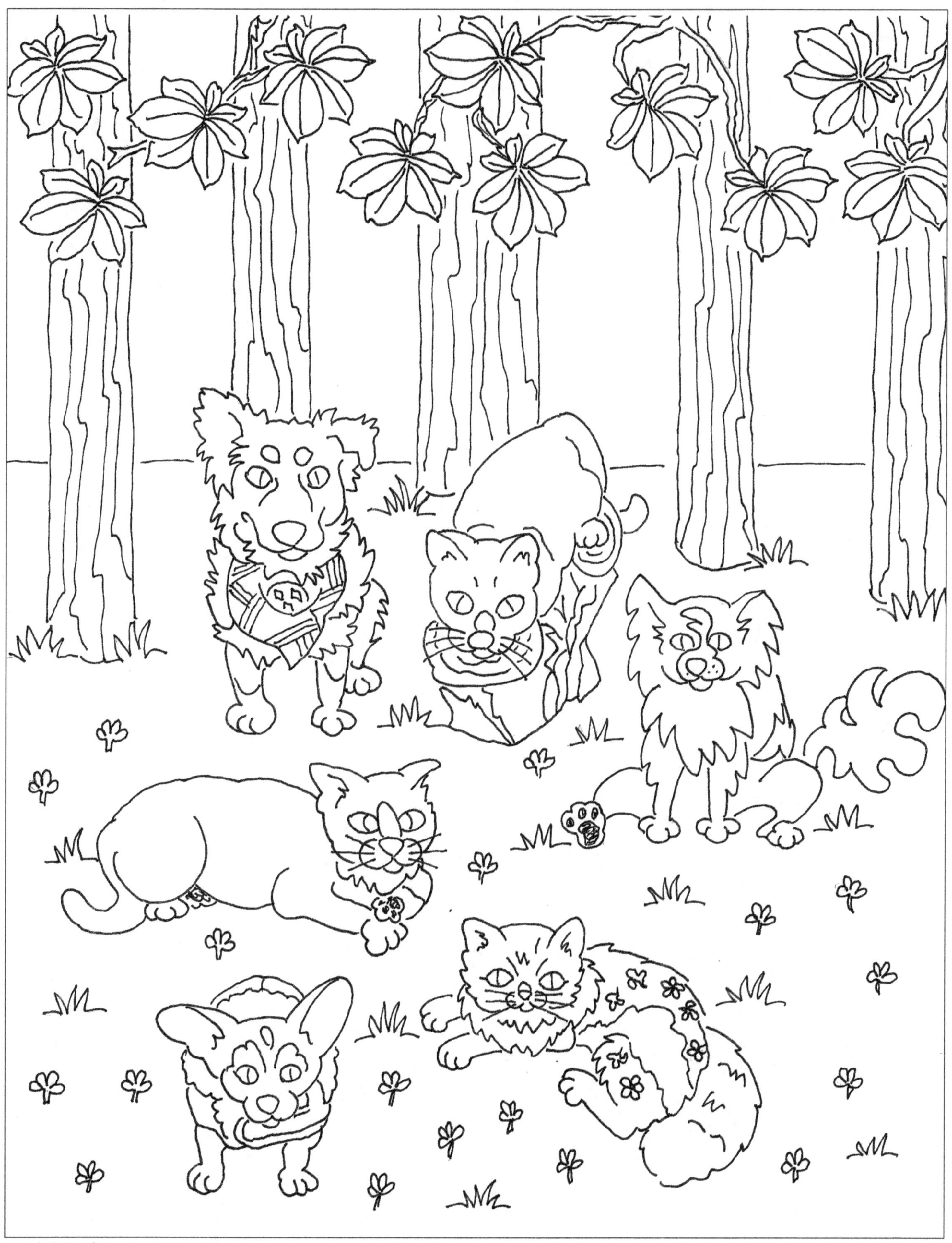

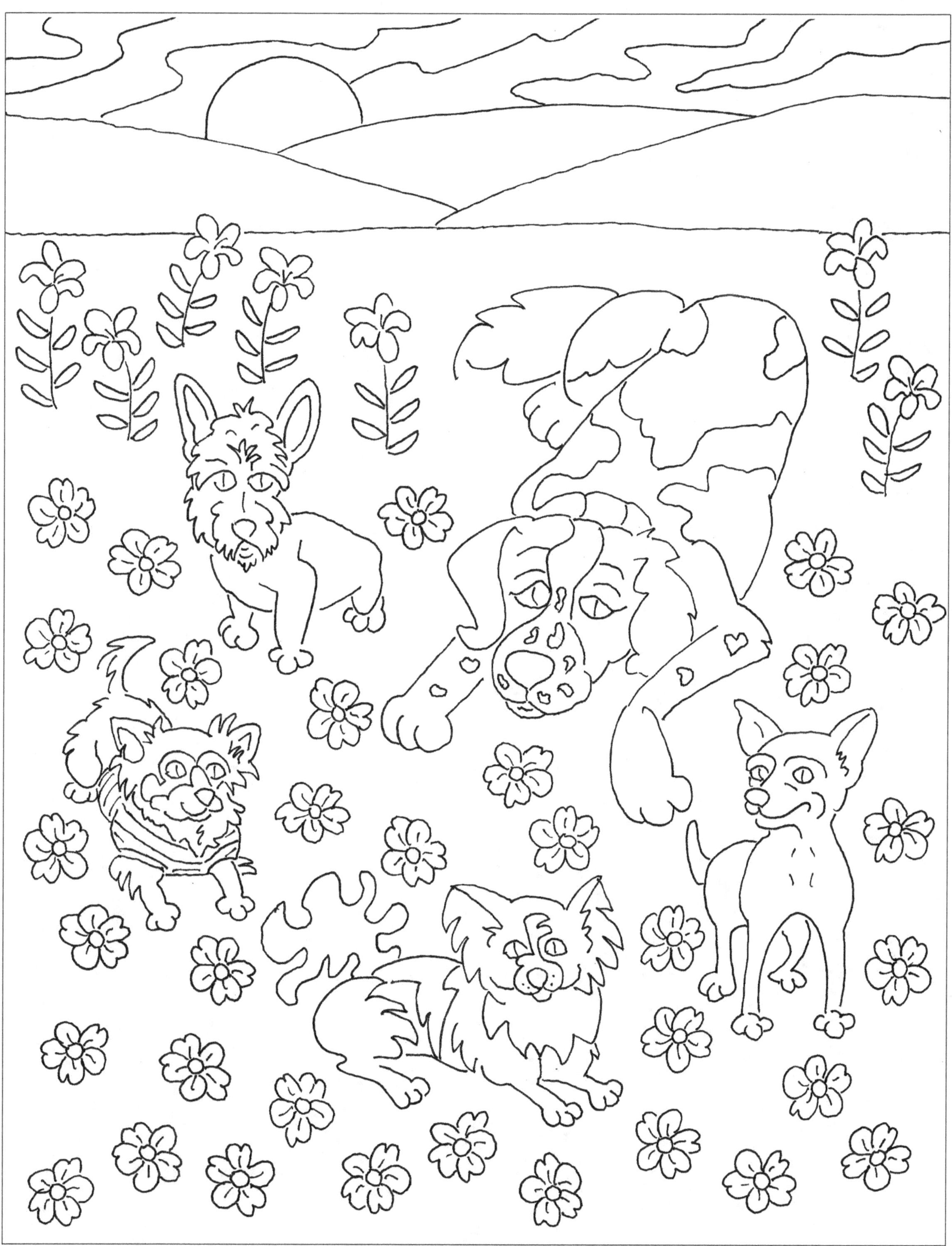

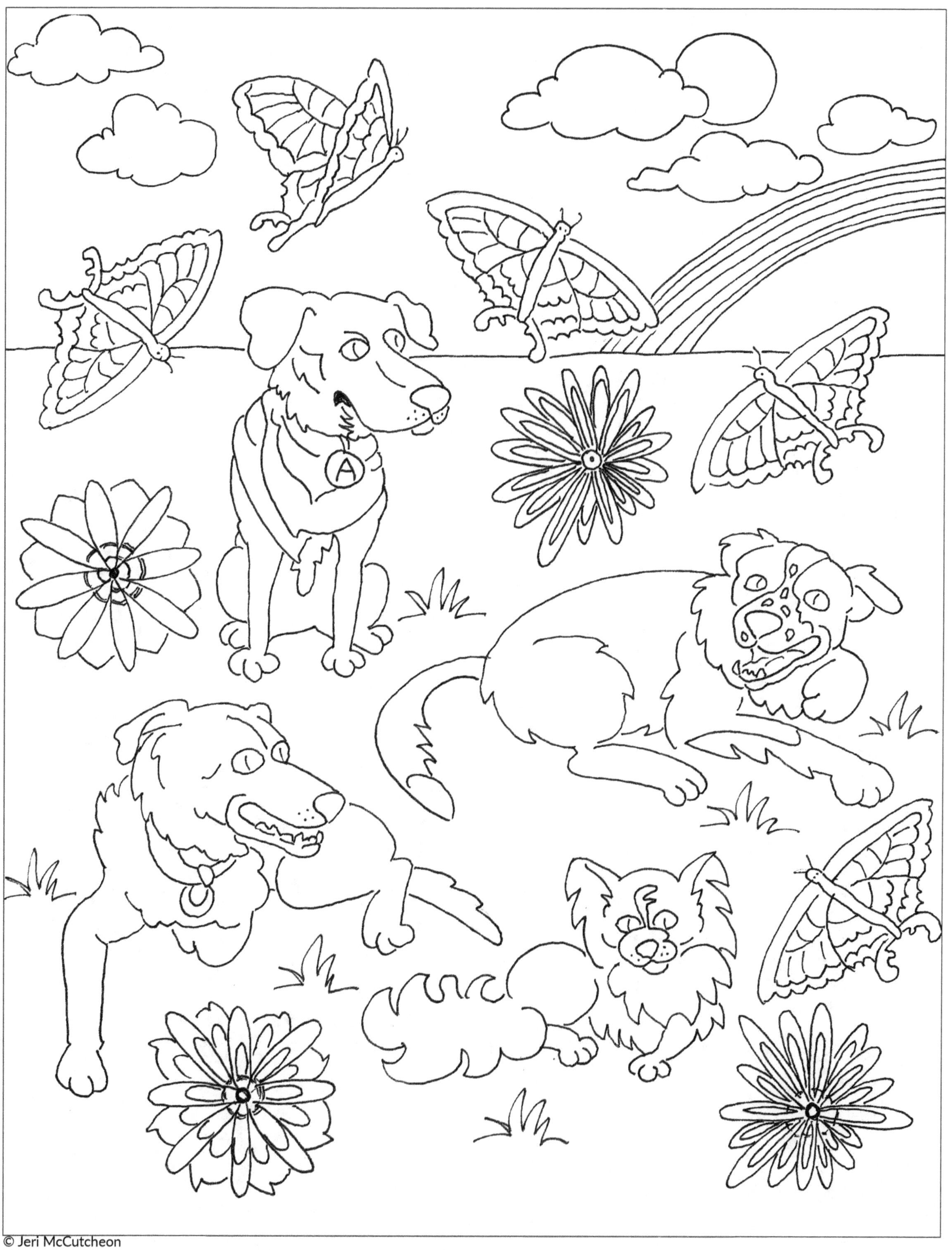

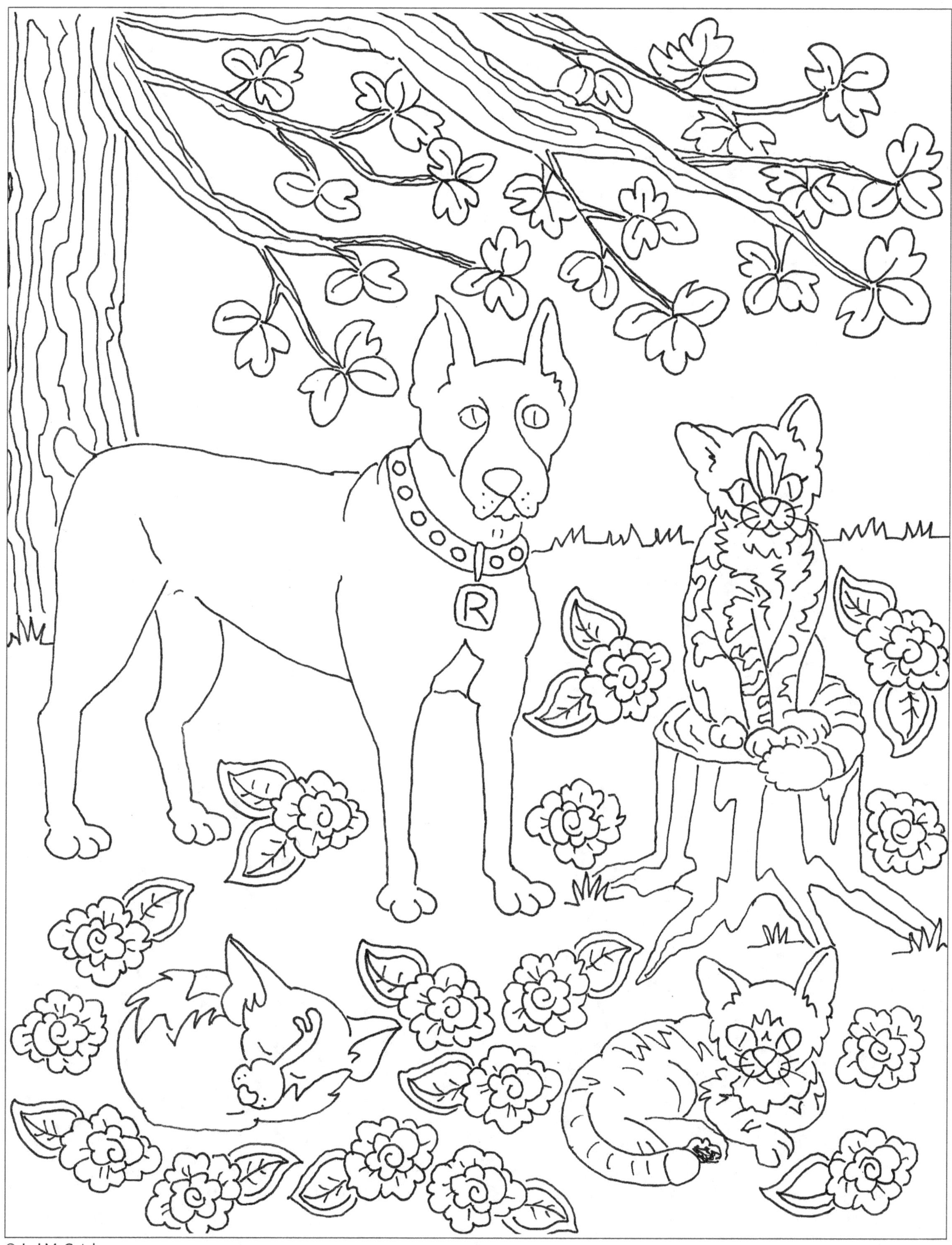

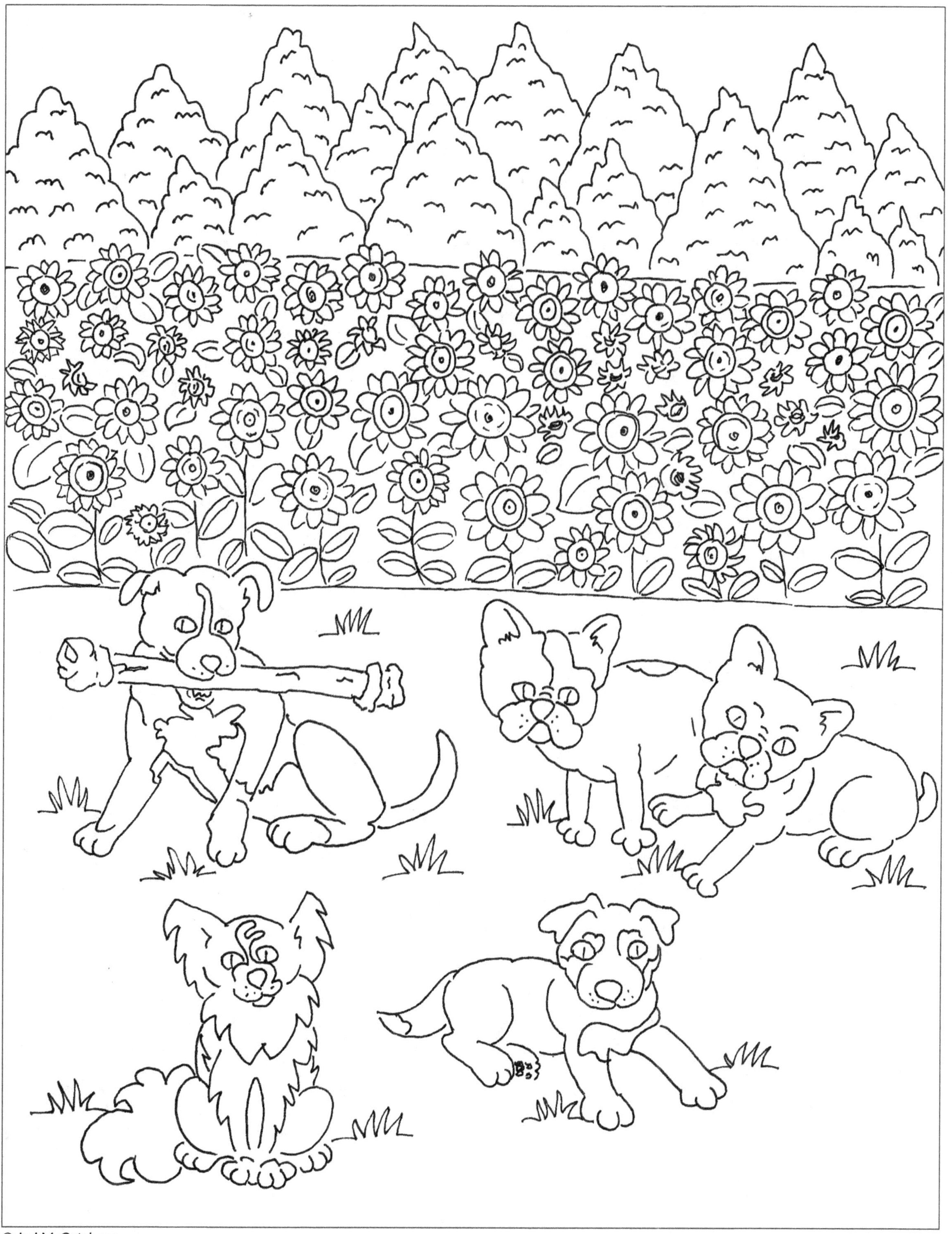

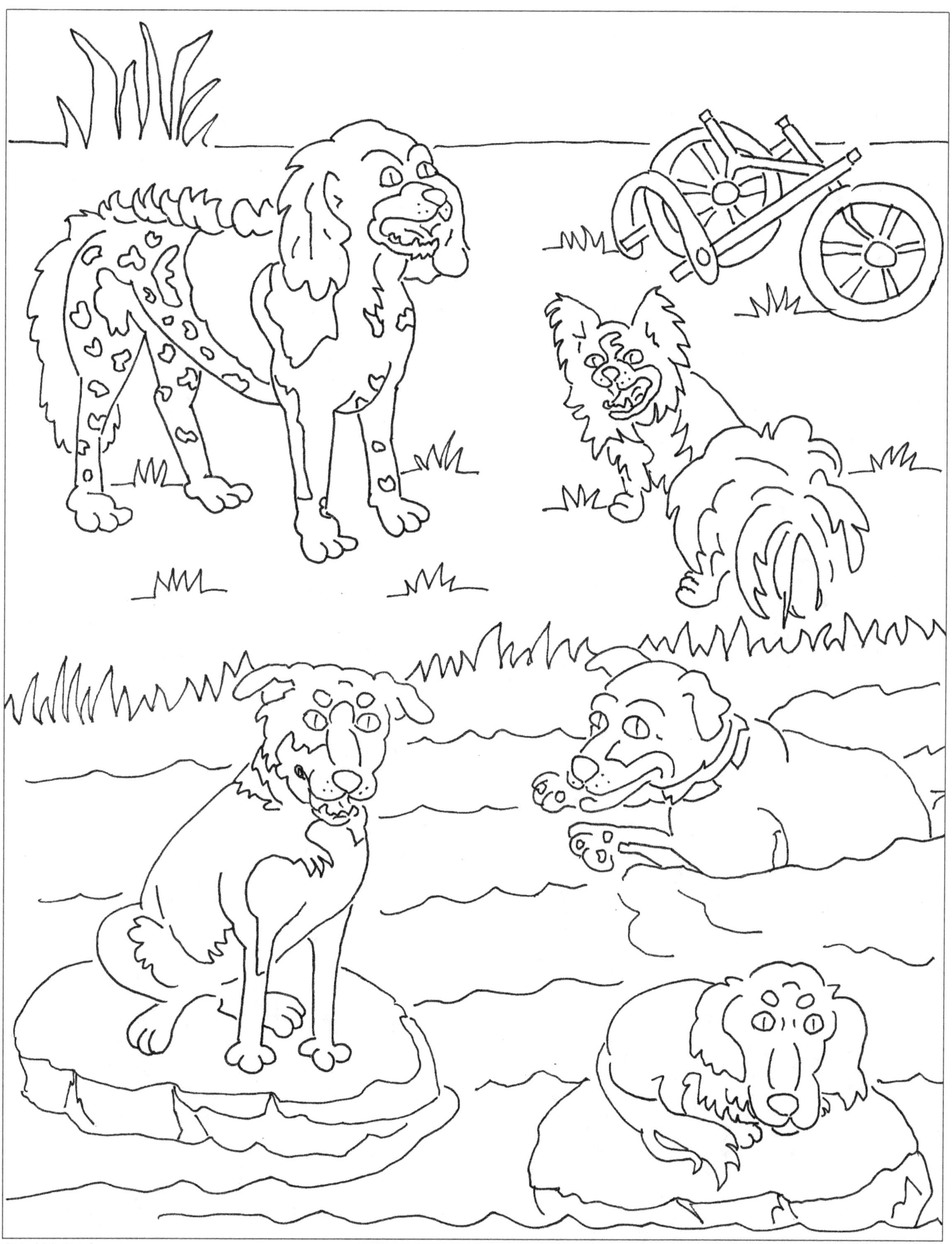

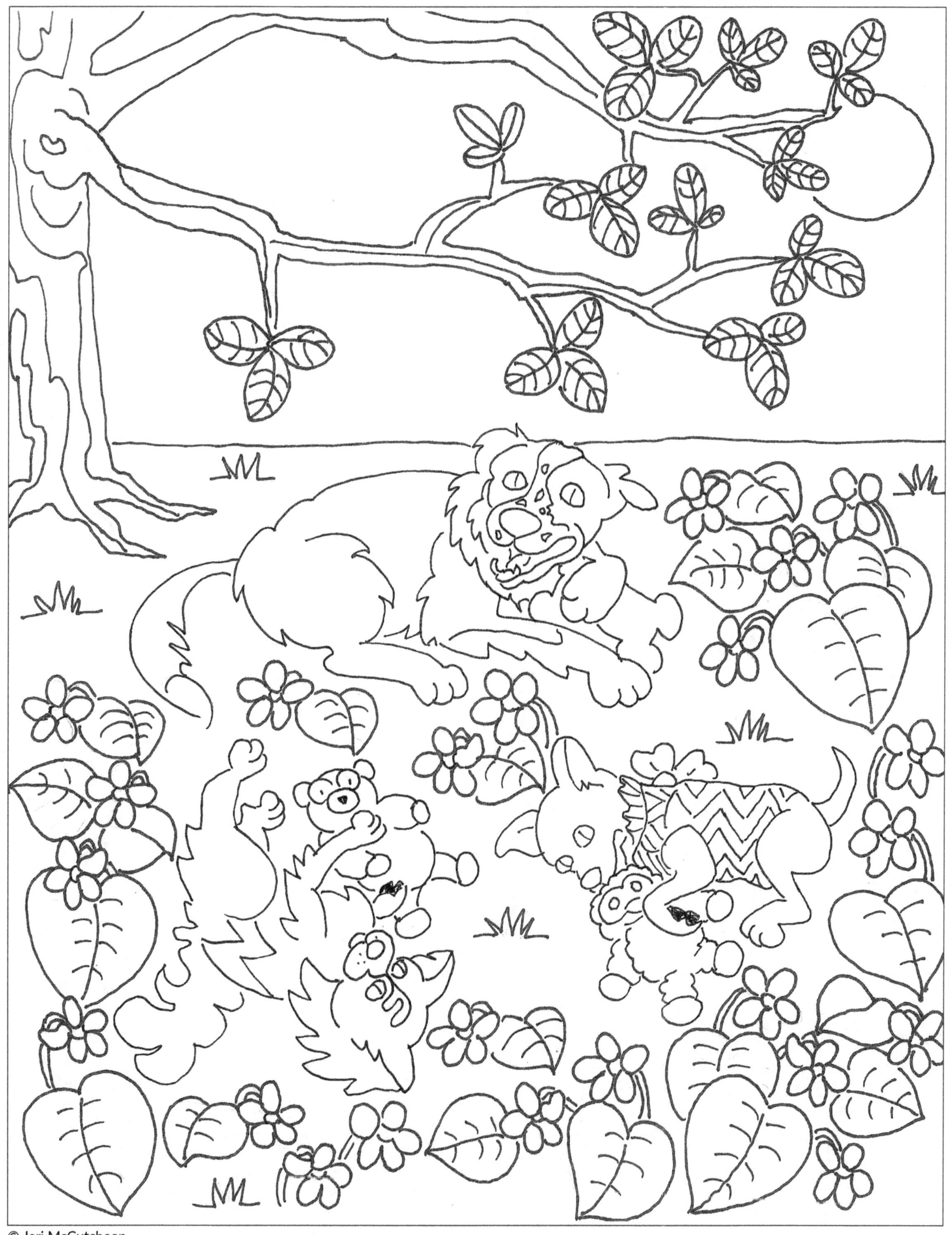

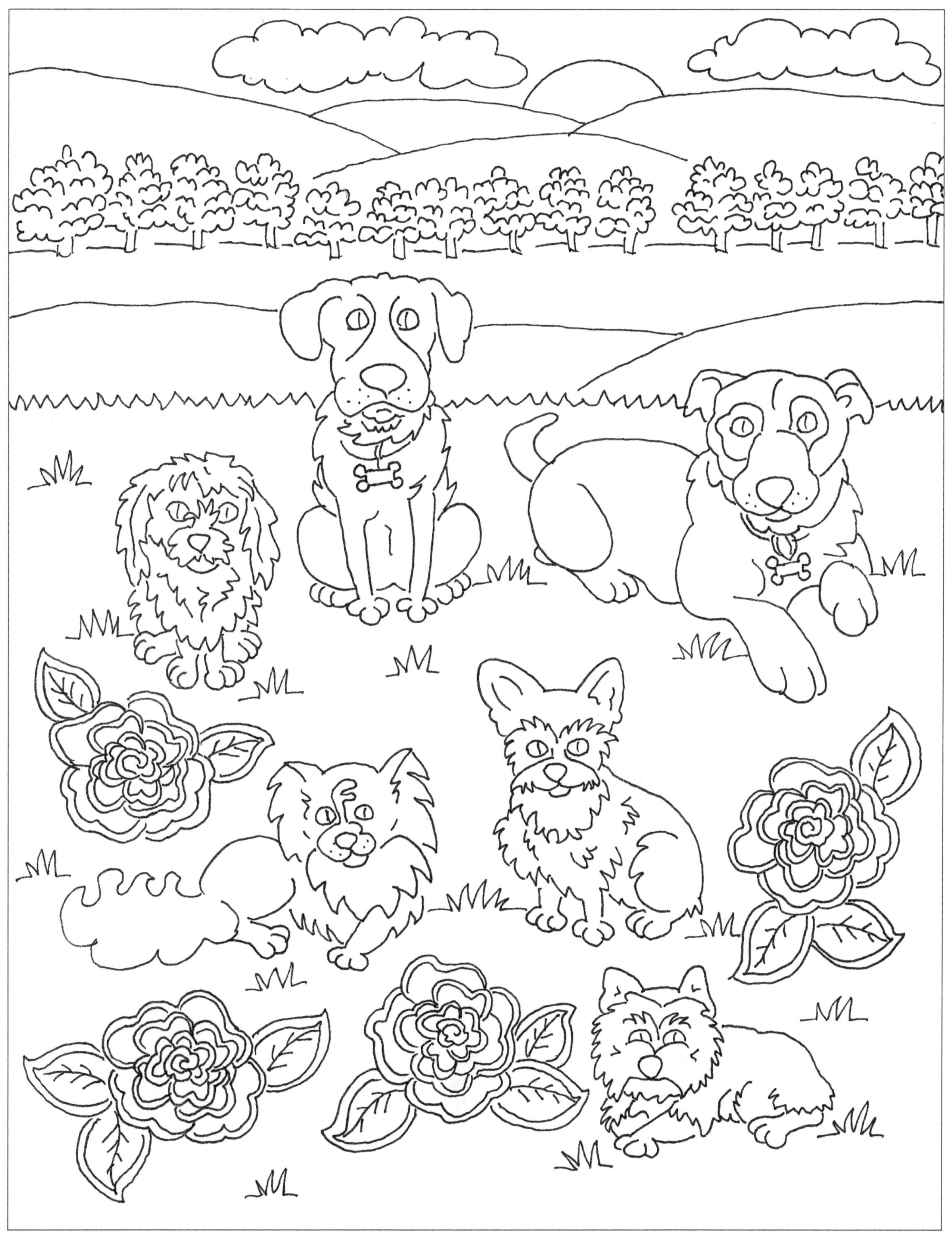

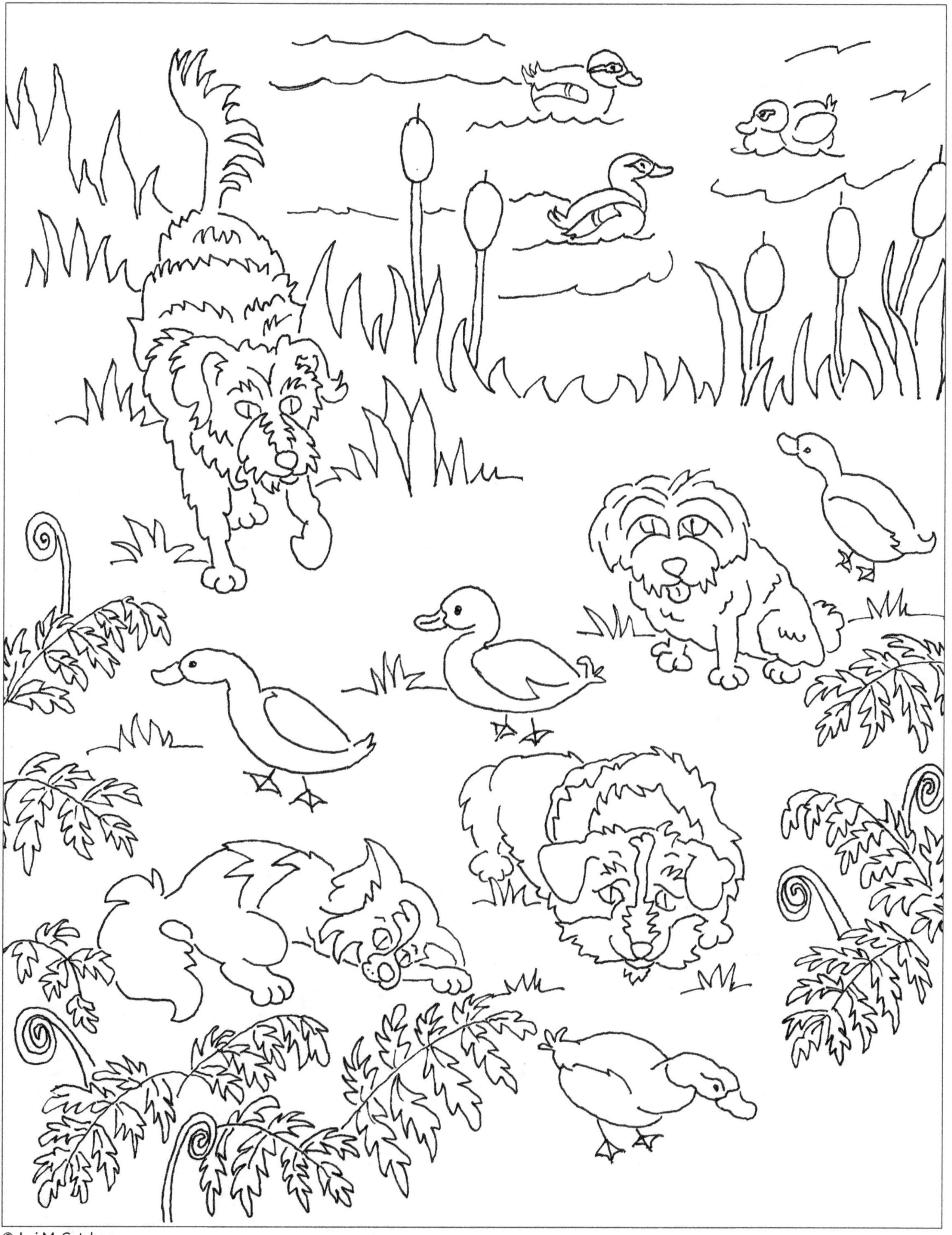

© Jeri McCutcheon

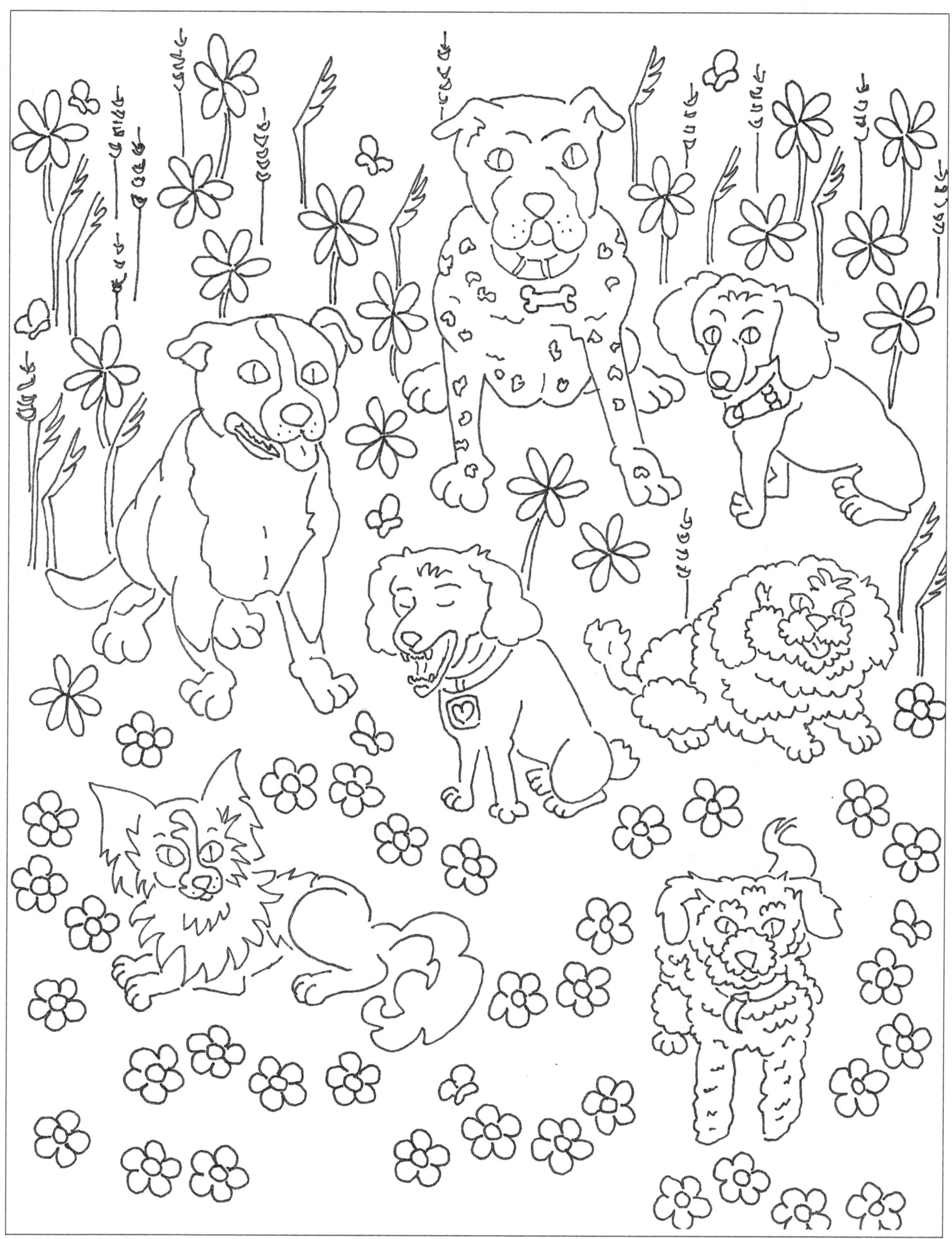

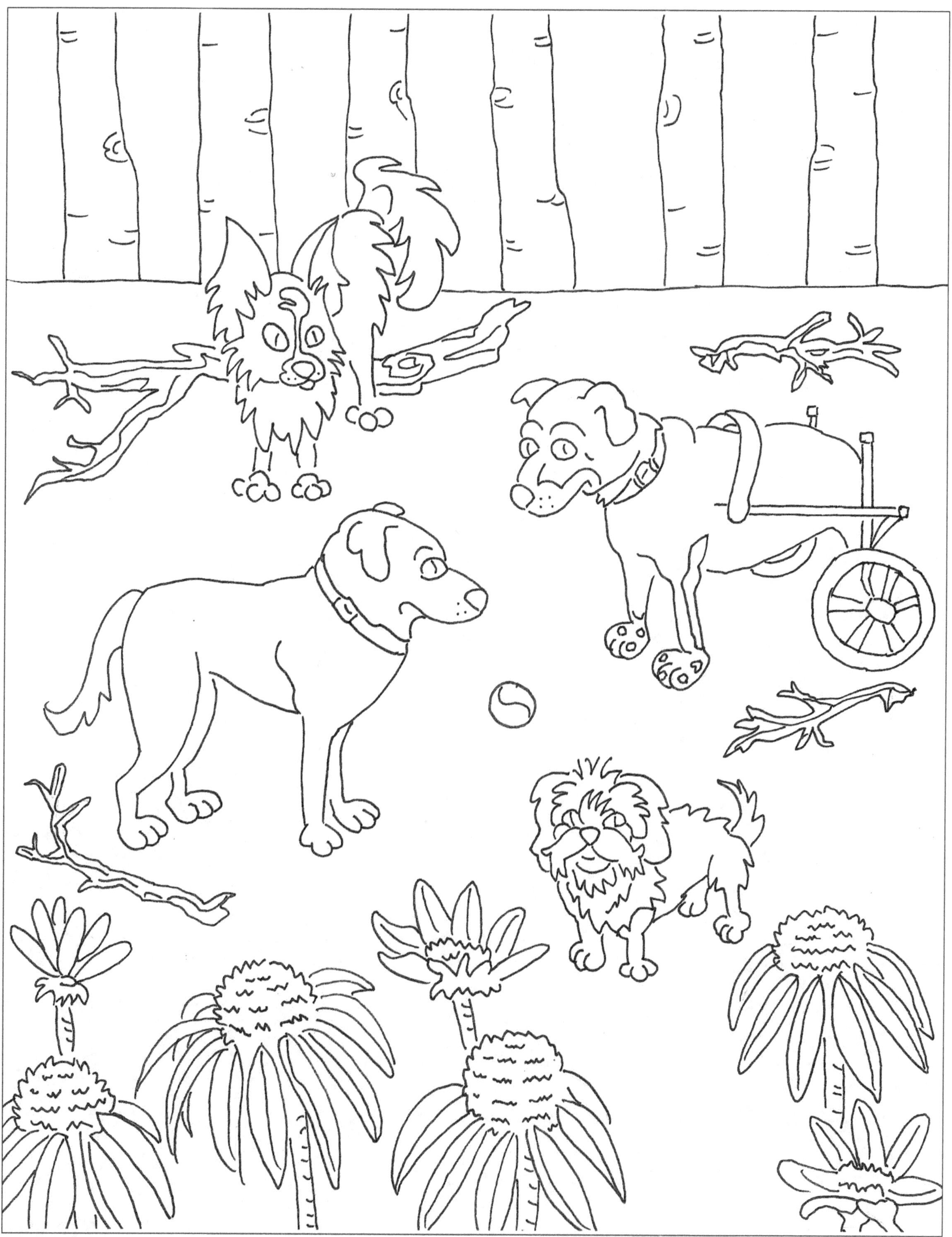

© Jeri McCutcheon

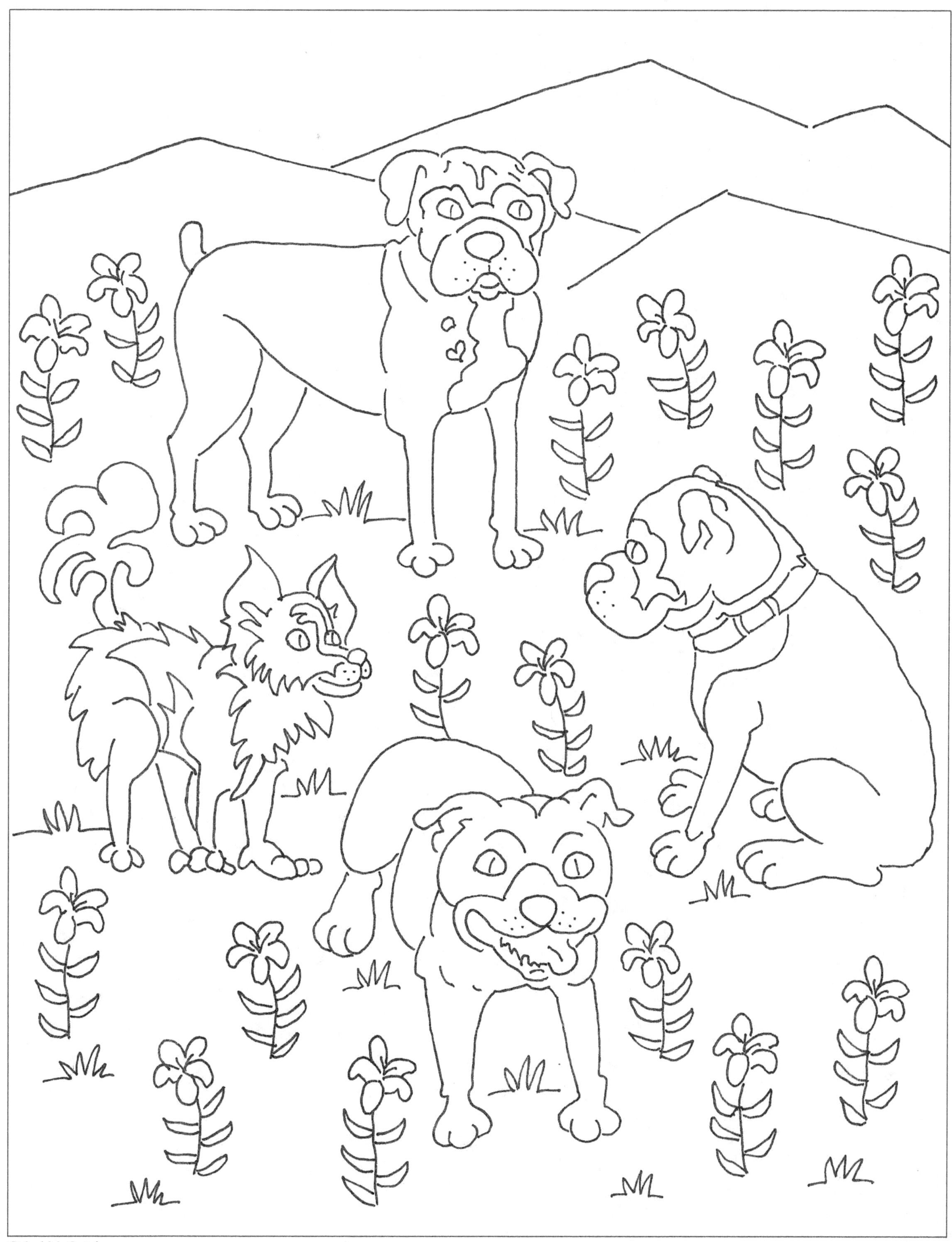

© Jeri McCutcheon

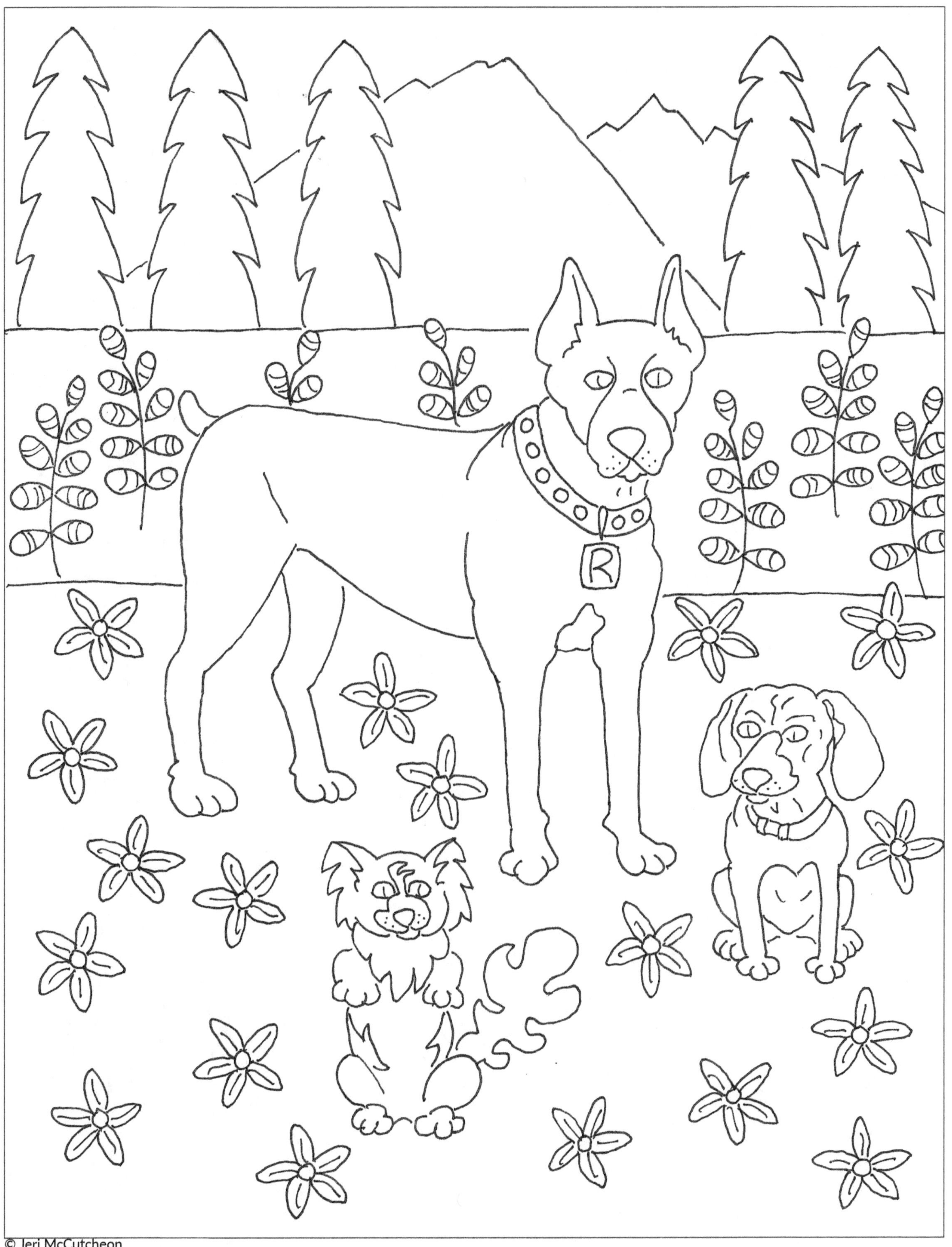

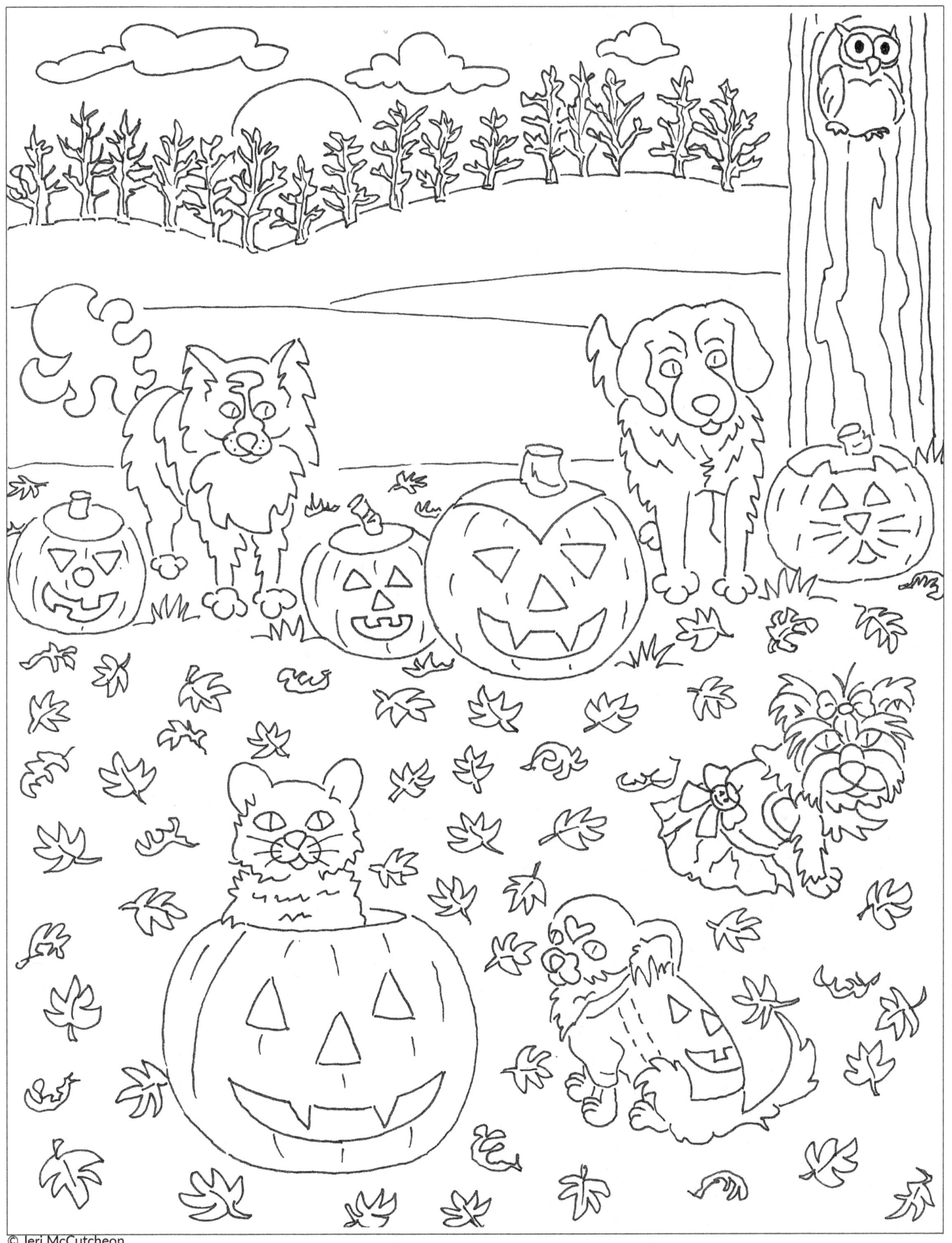

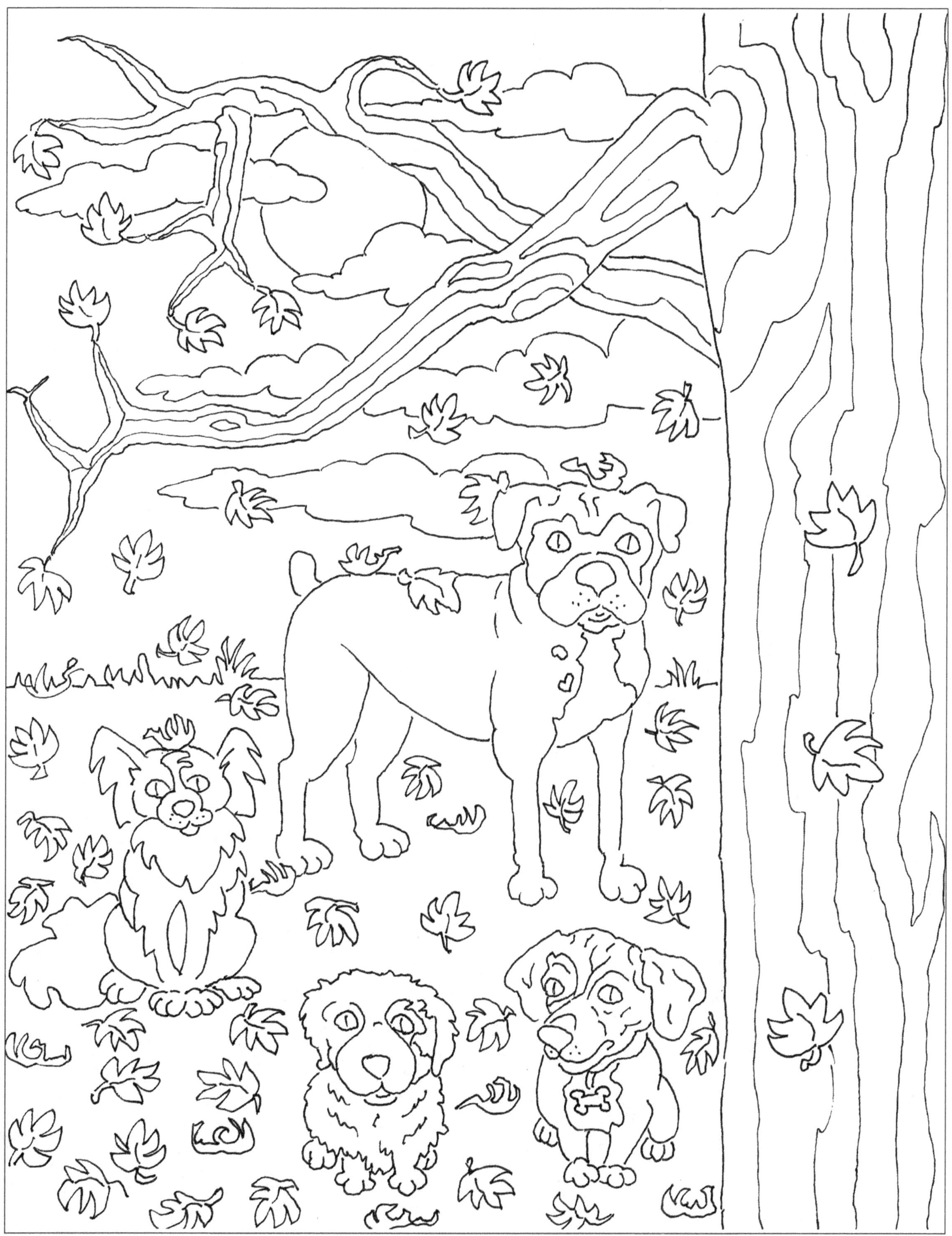

© Jeri McCutcheon

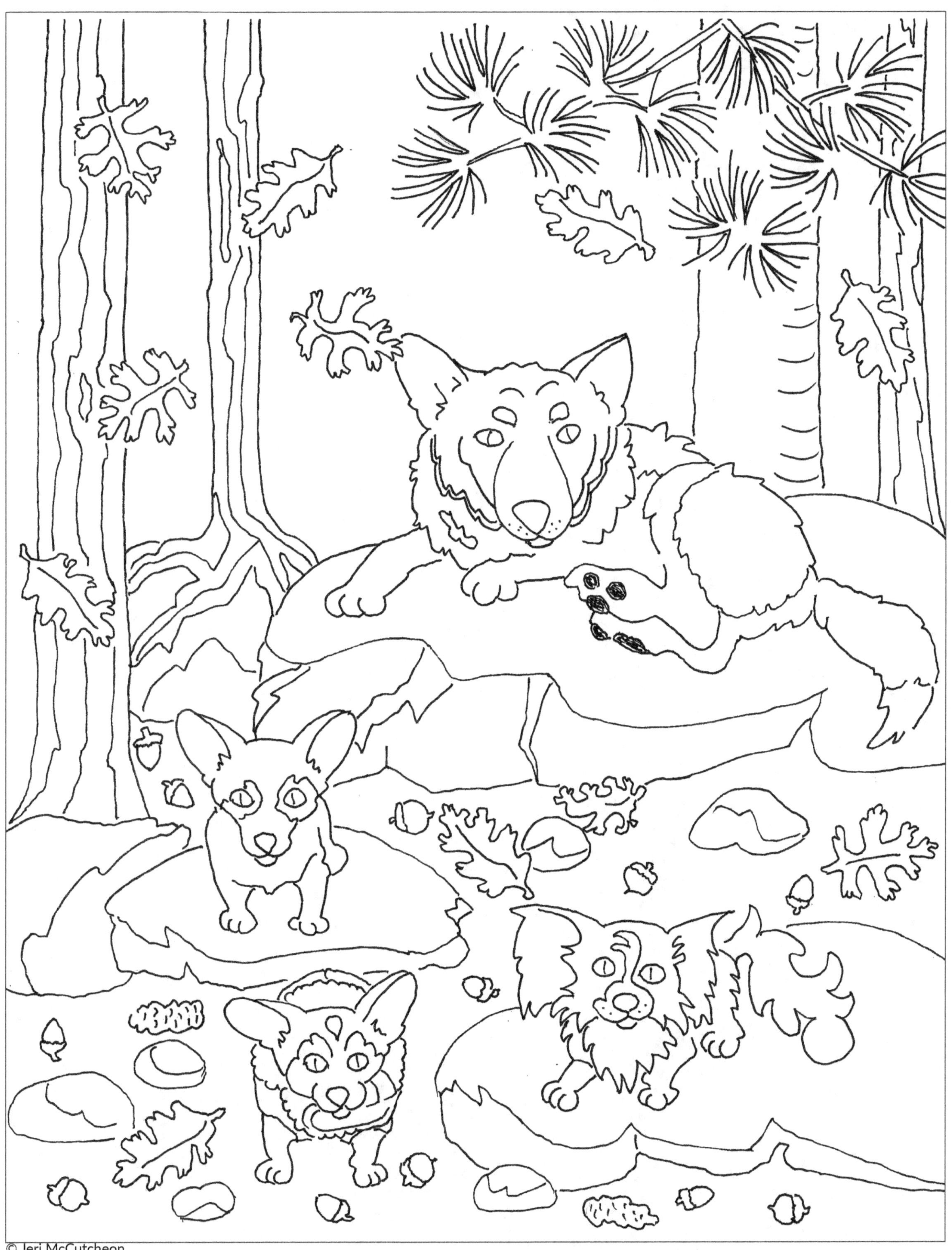

© Jeri McCutcheon

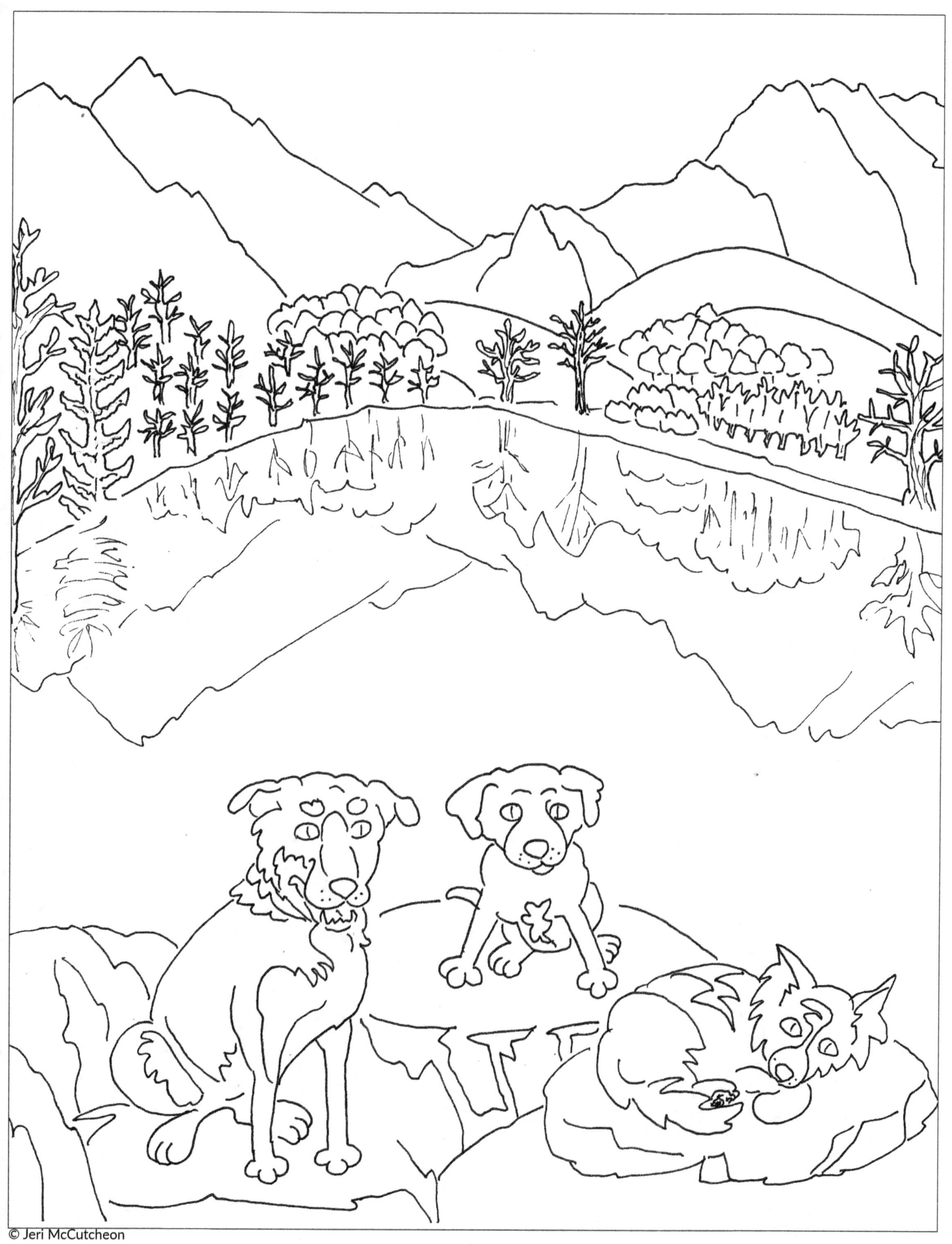

© Jeri McCutcheon

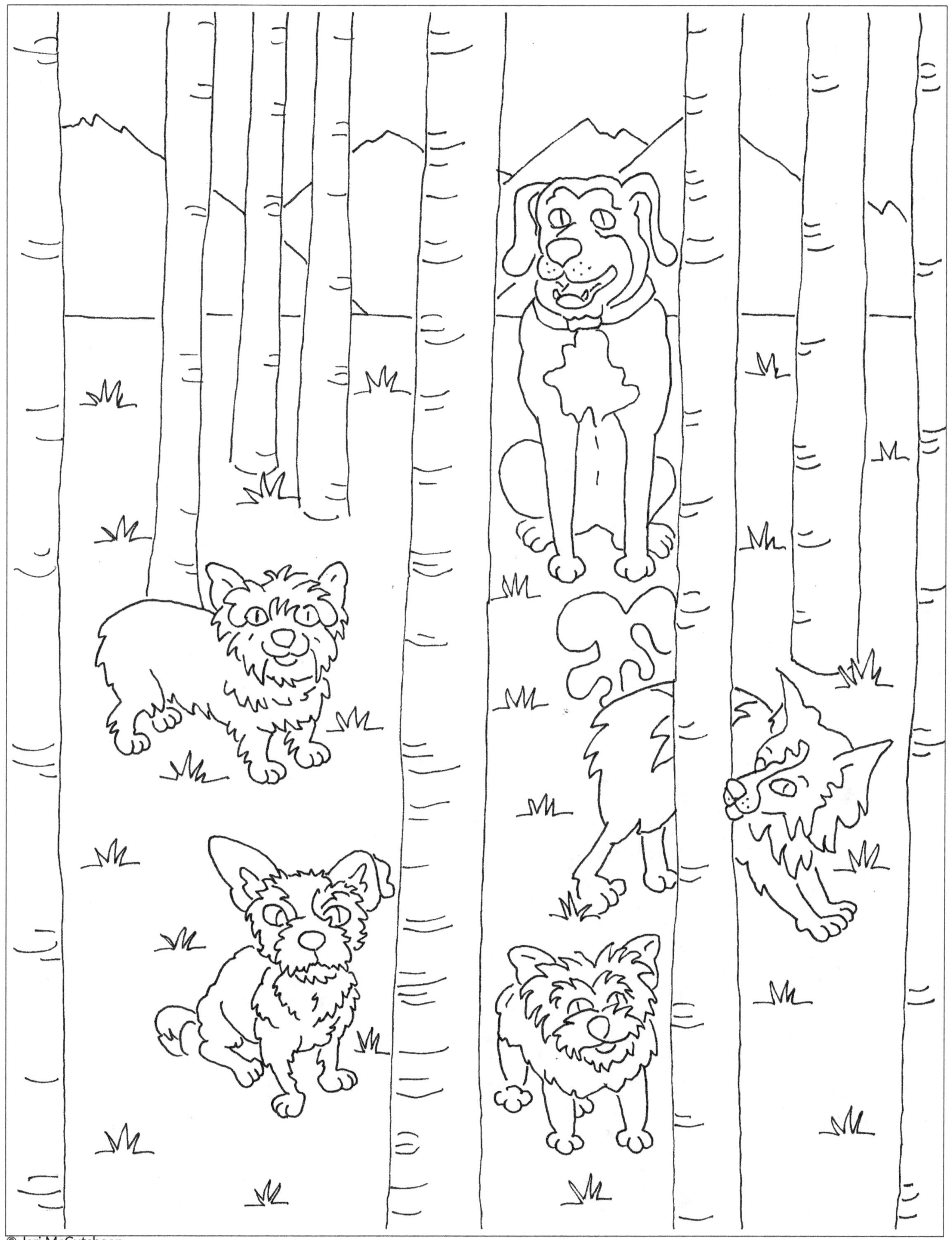

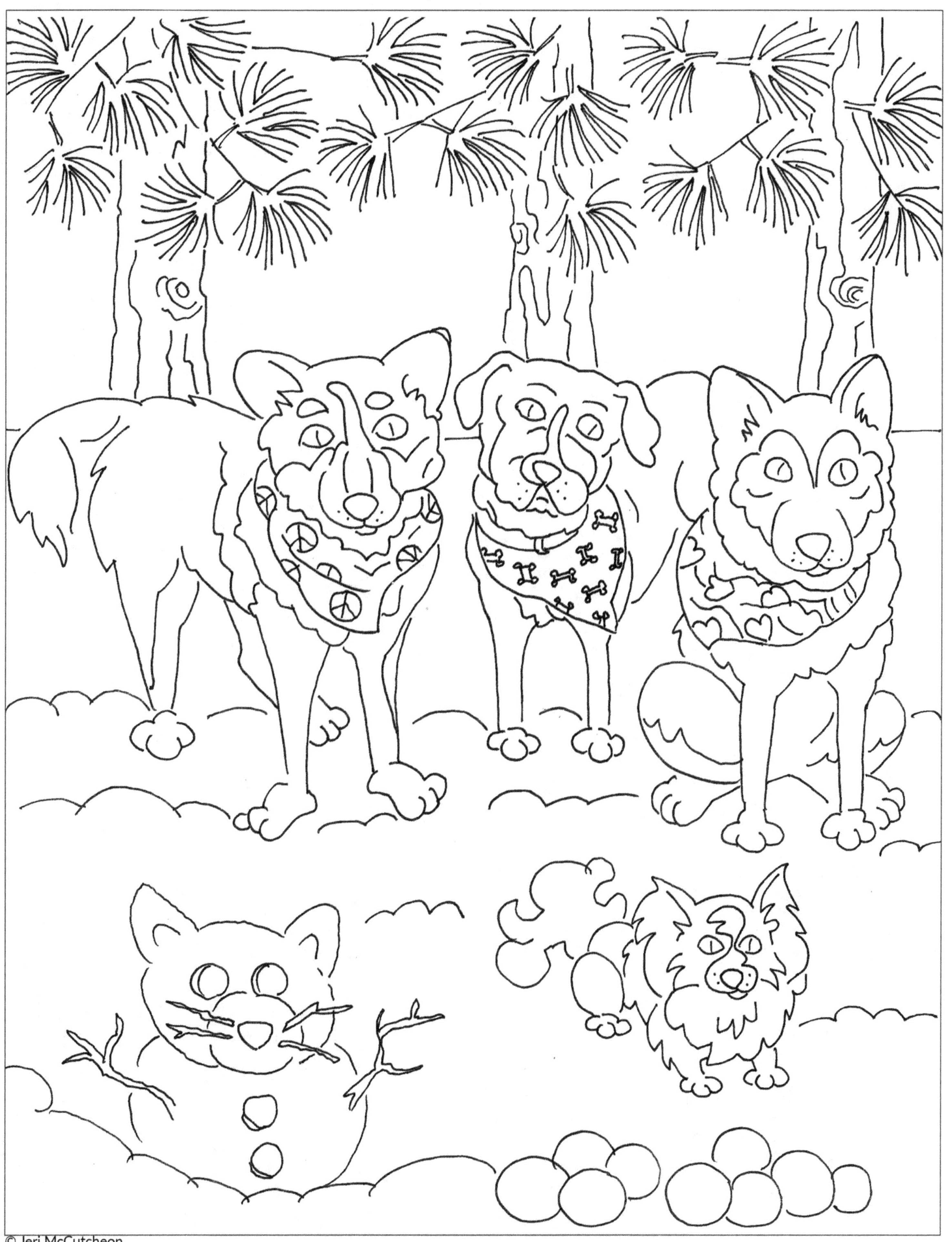

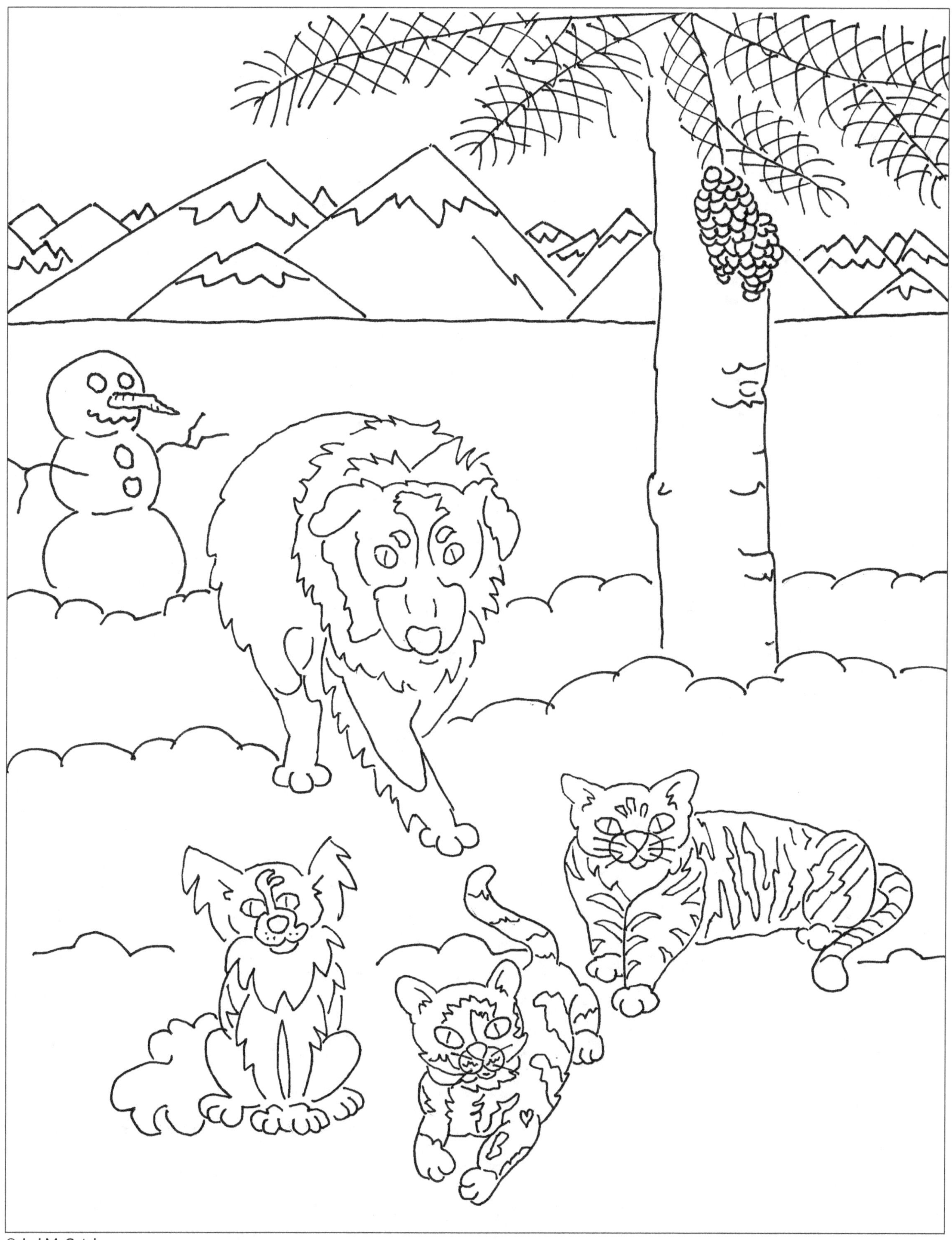

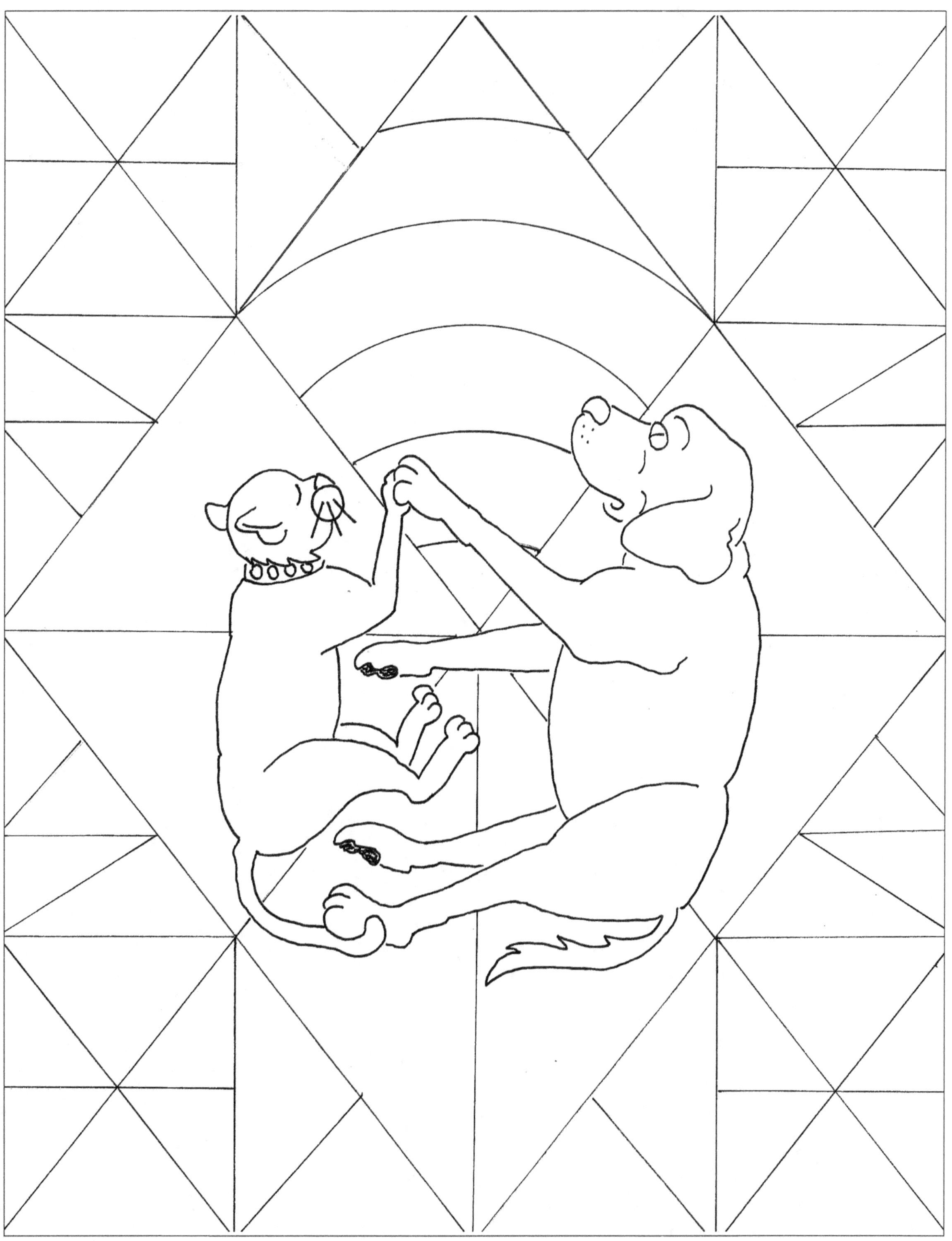

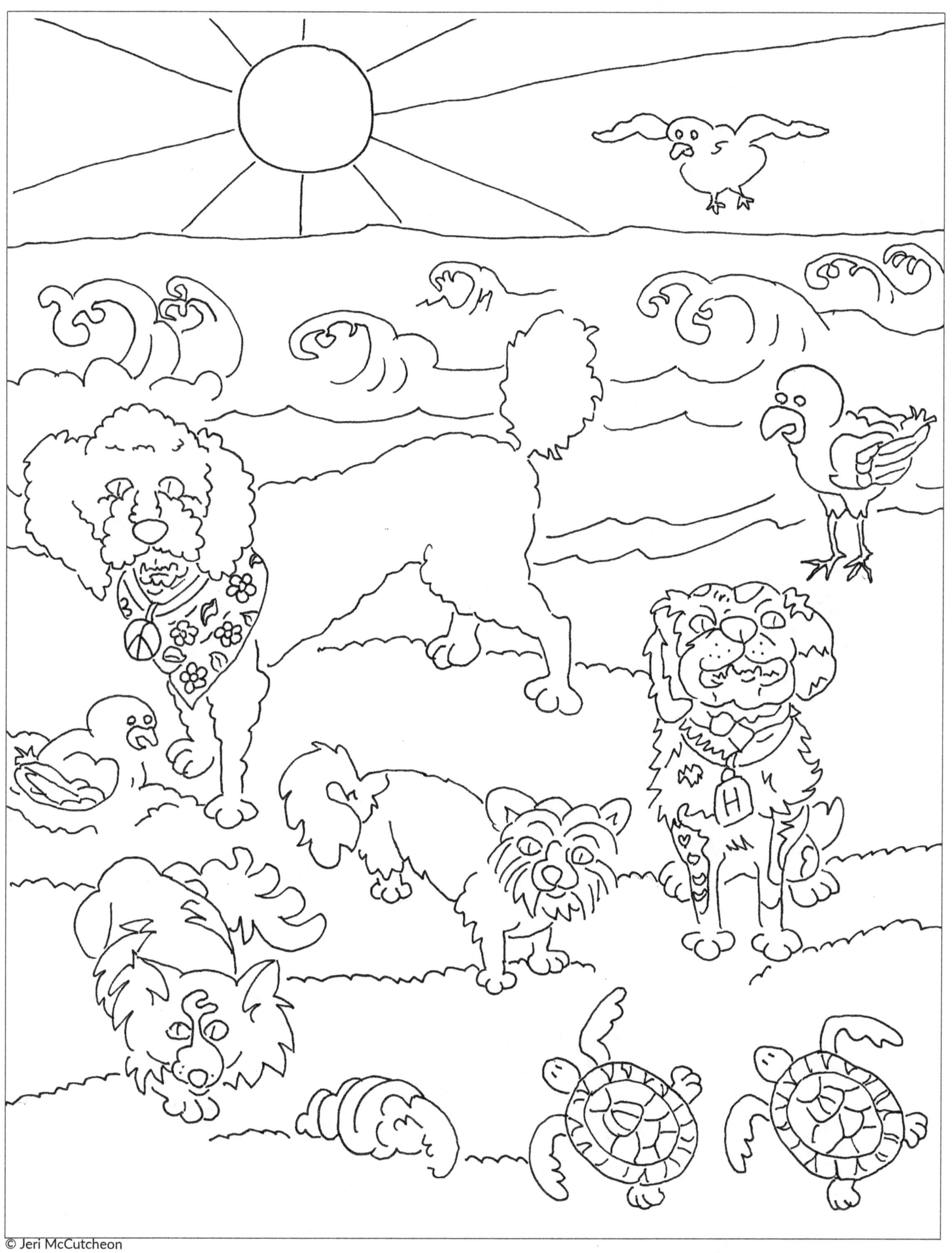

© Jeri McCutcheon

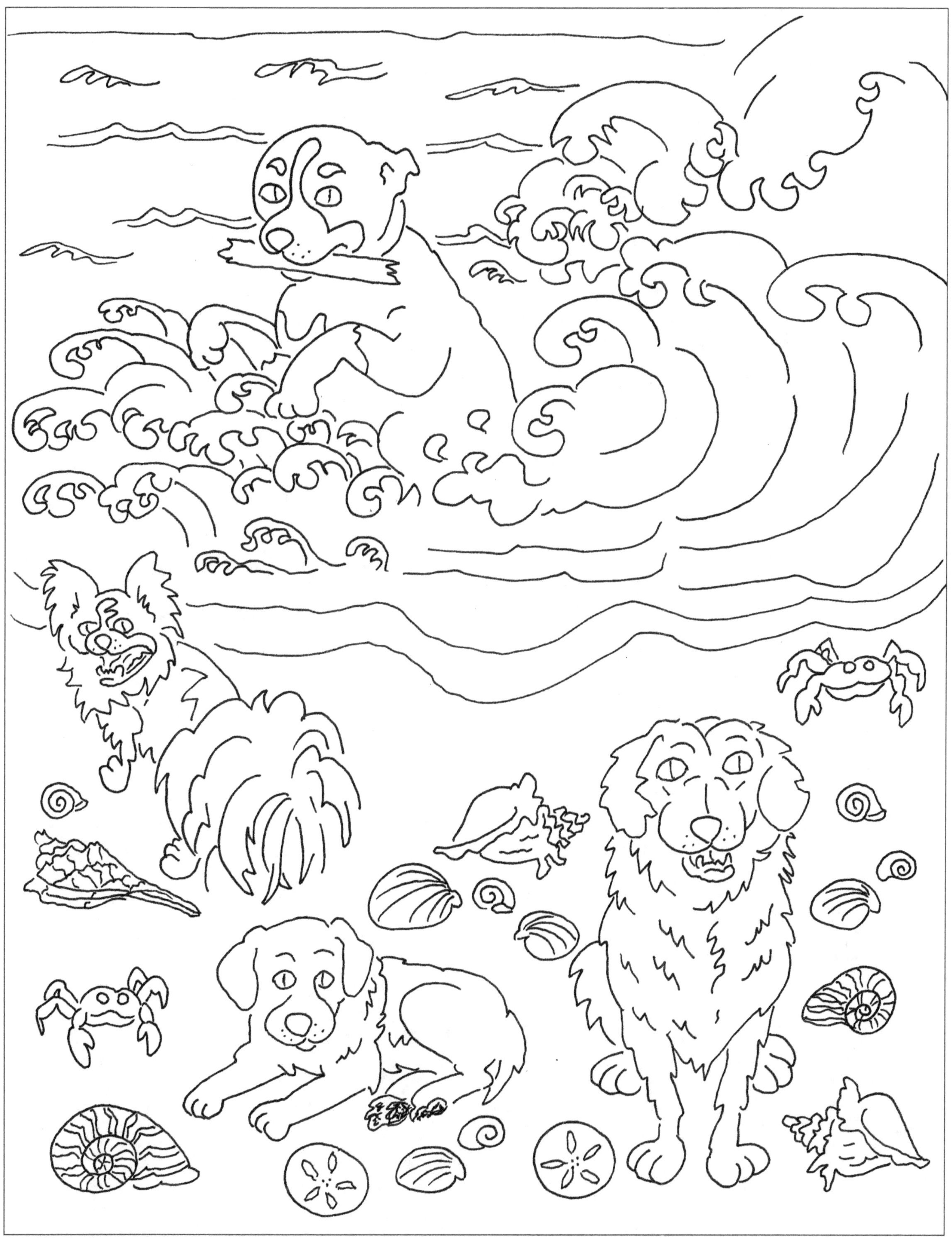

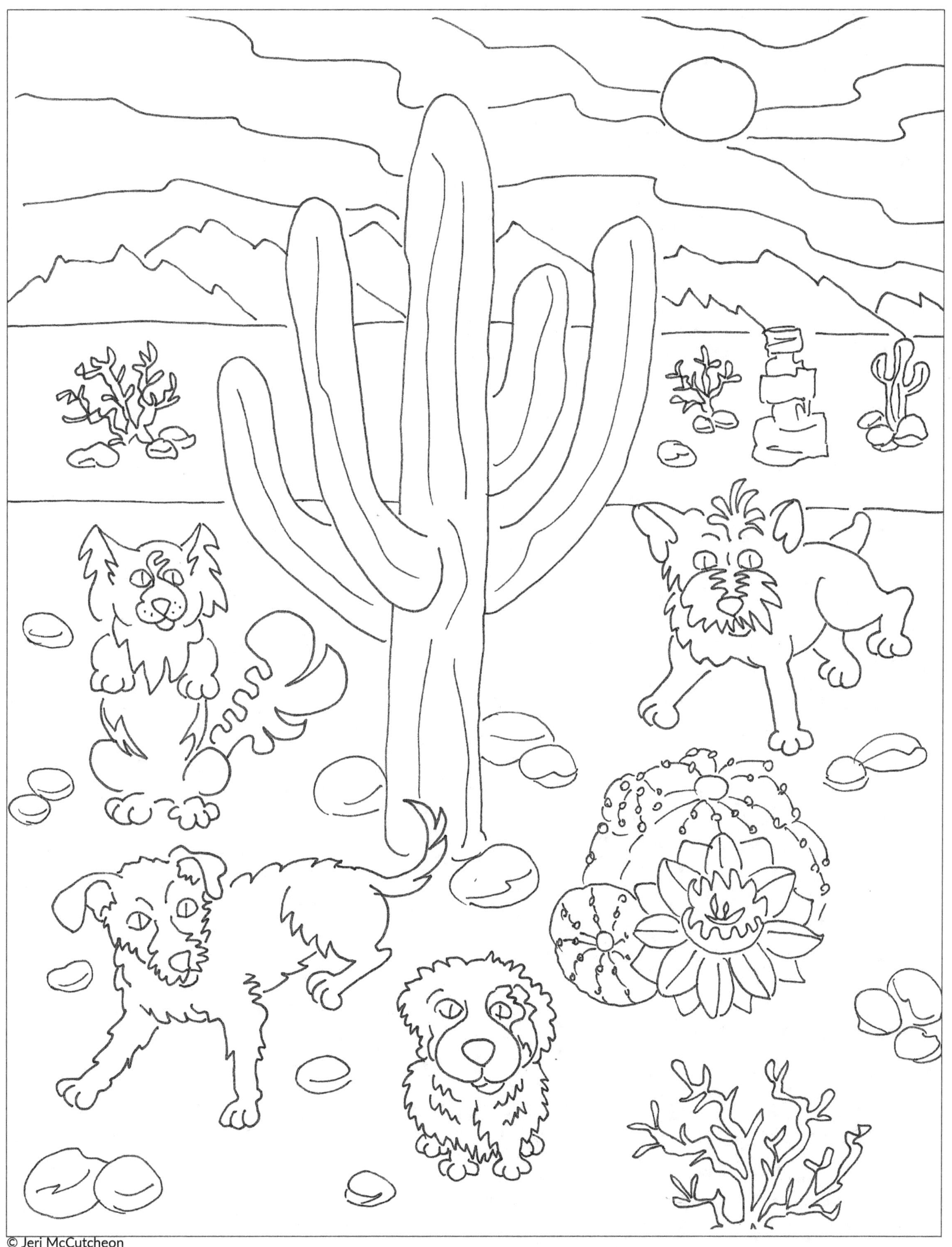

© Jeri McCutcheon

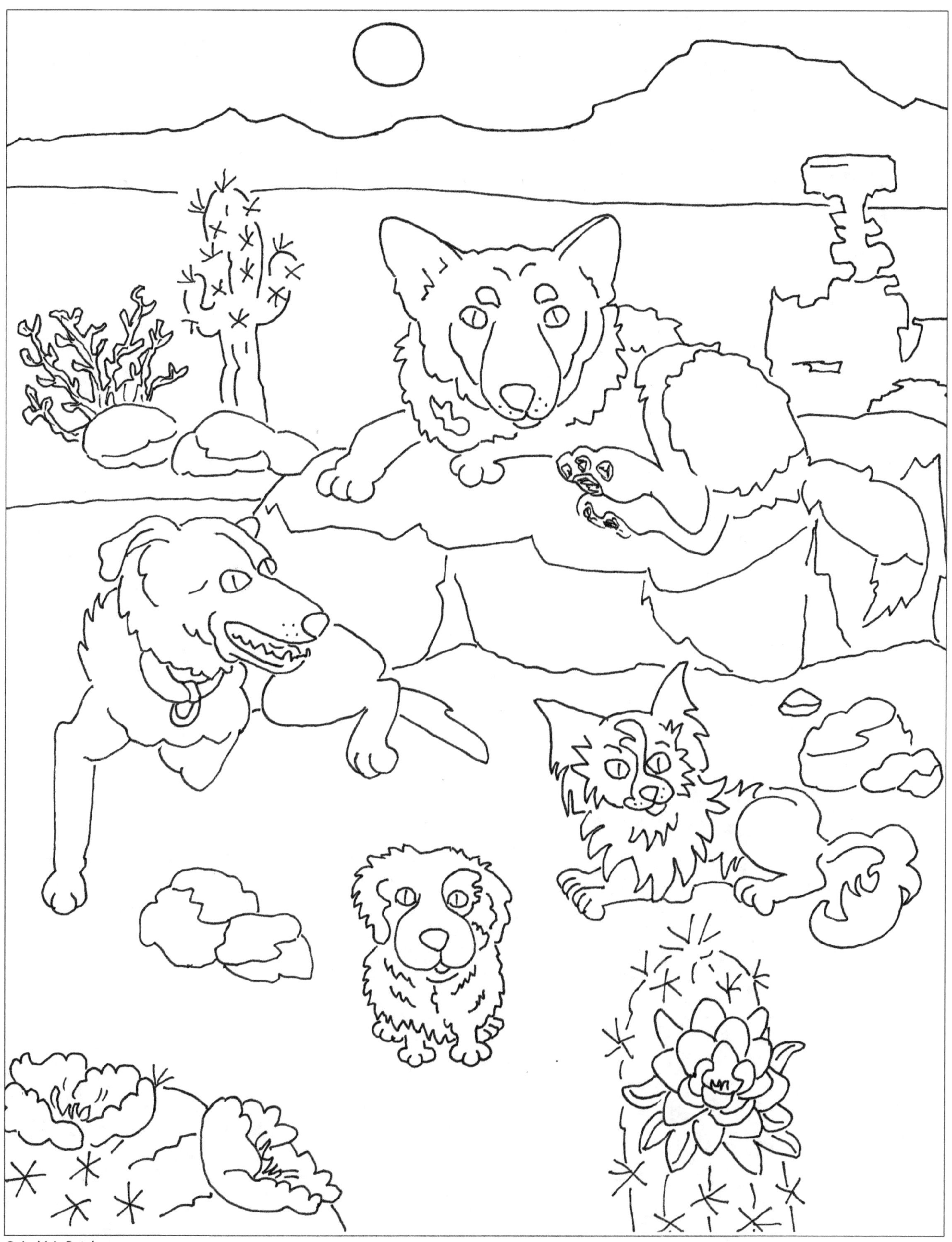

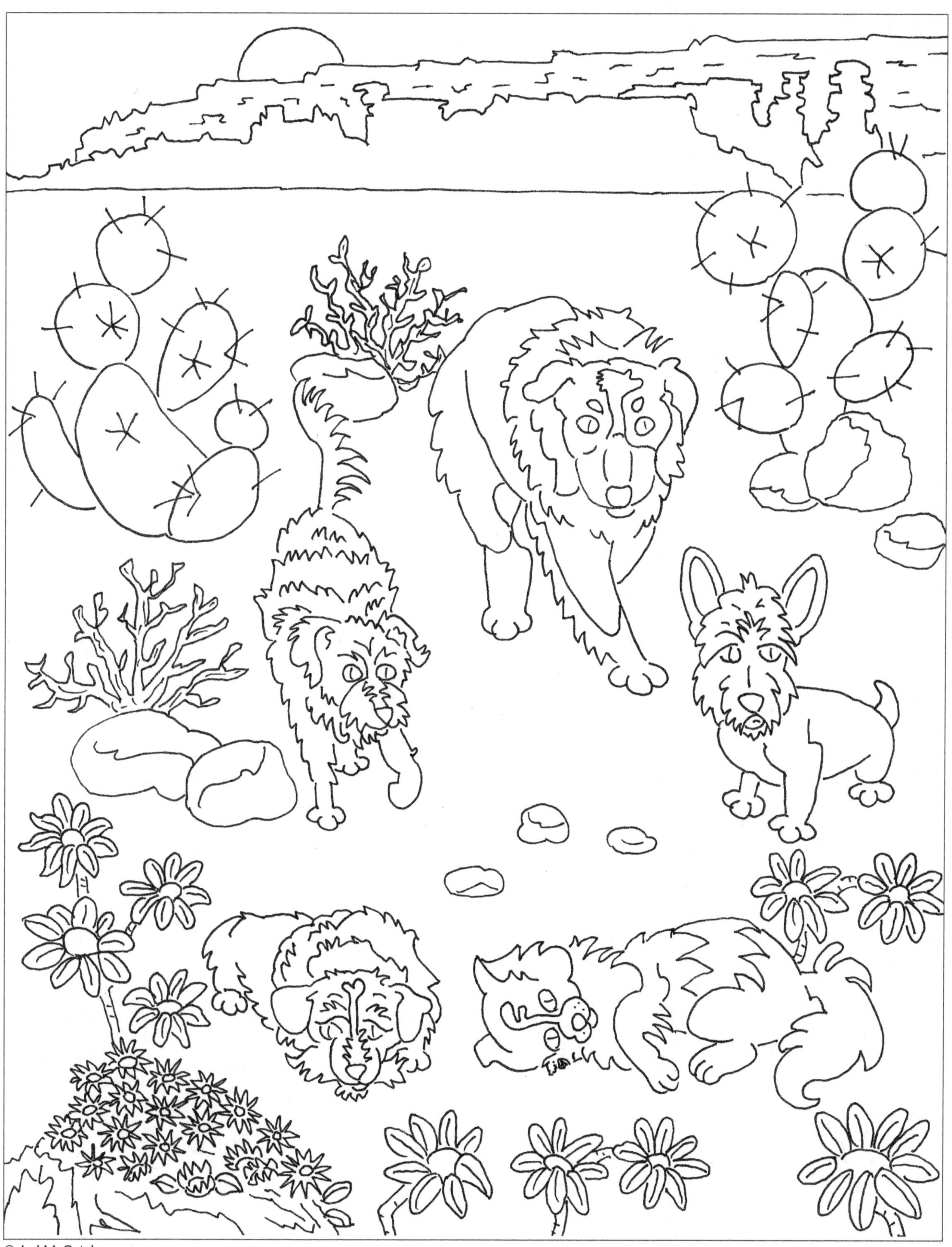

© Jeri McCutcheon

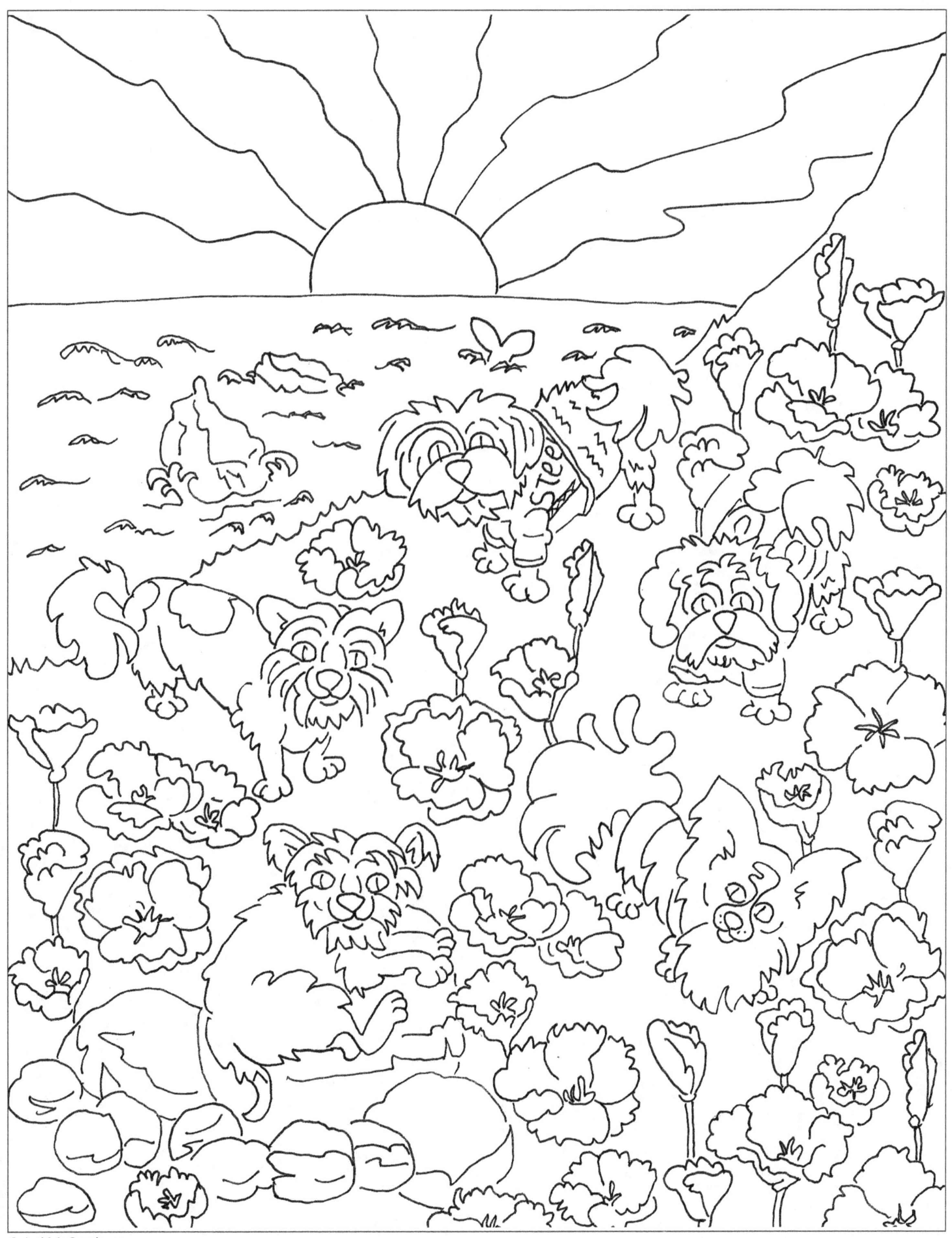

© Jeri McCutcheon

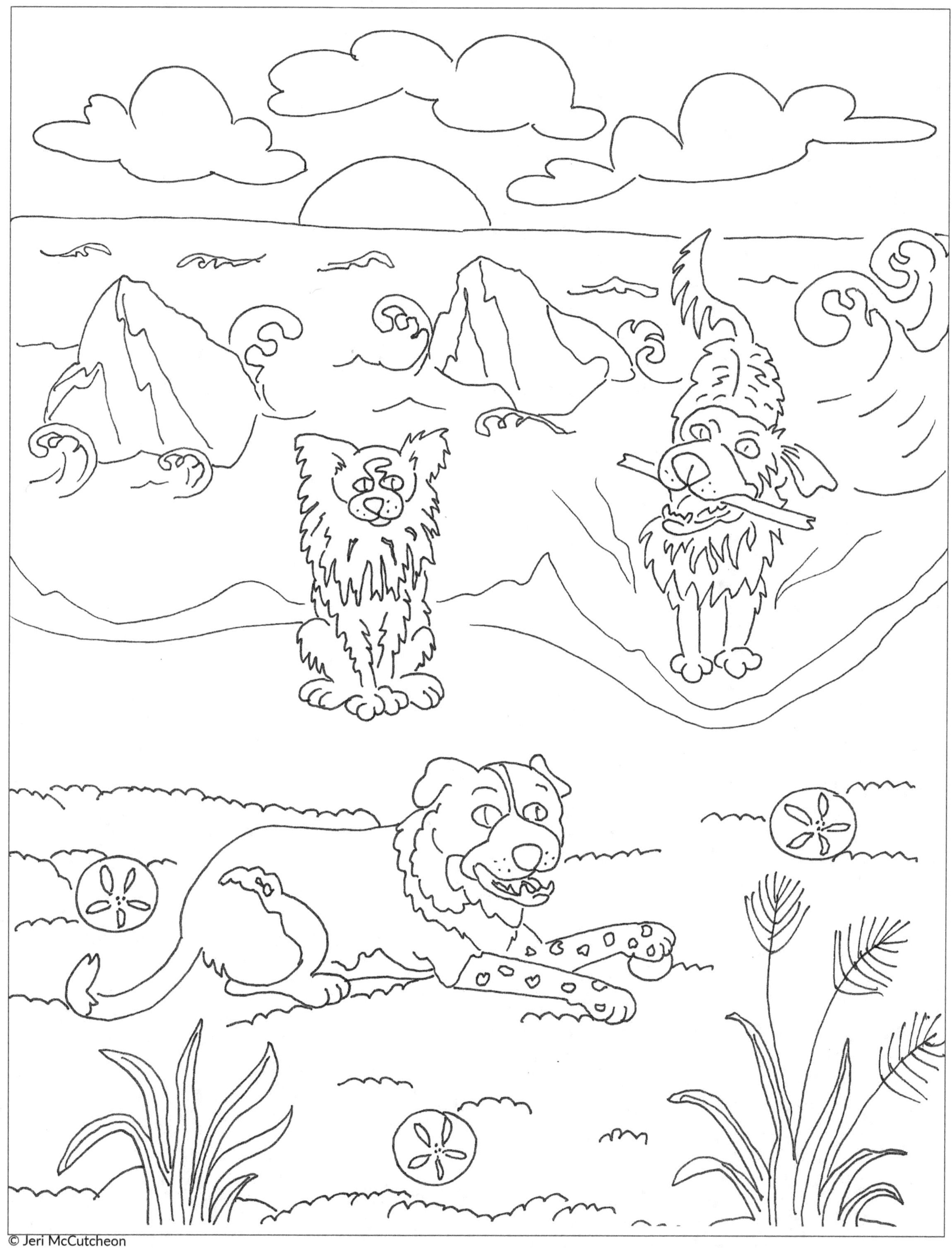

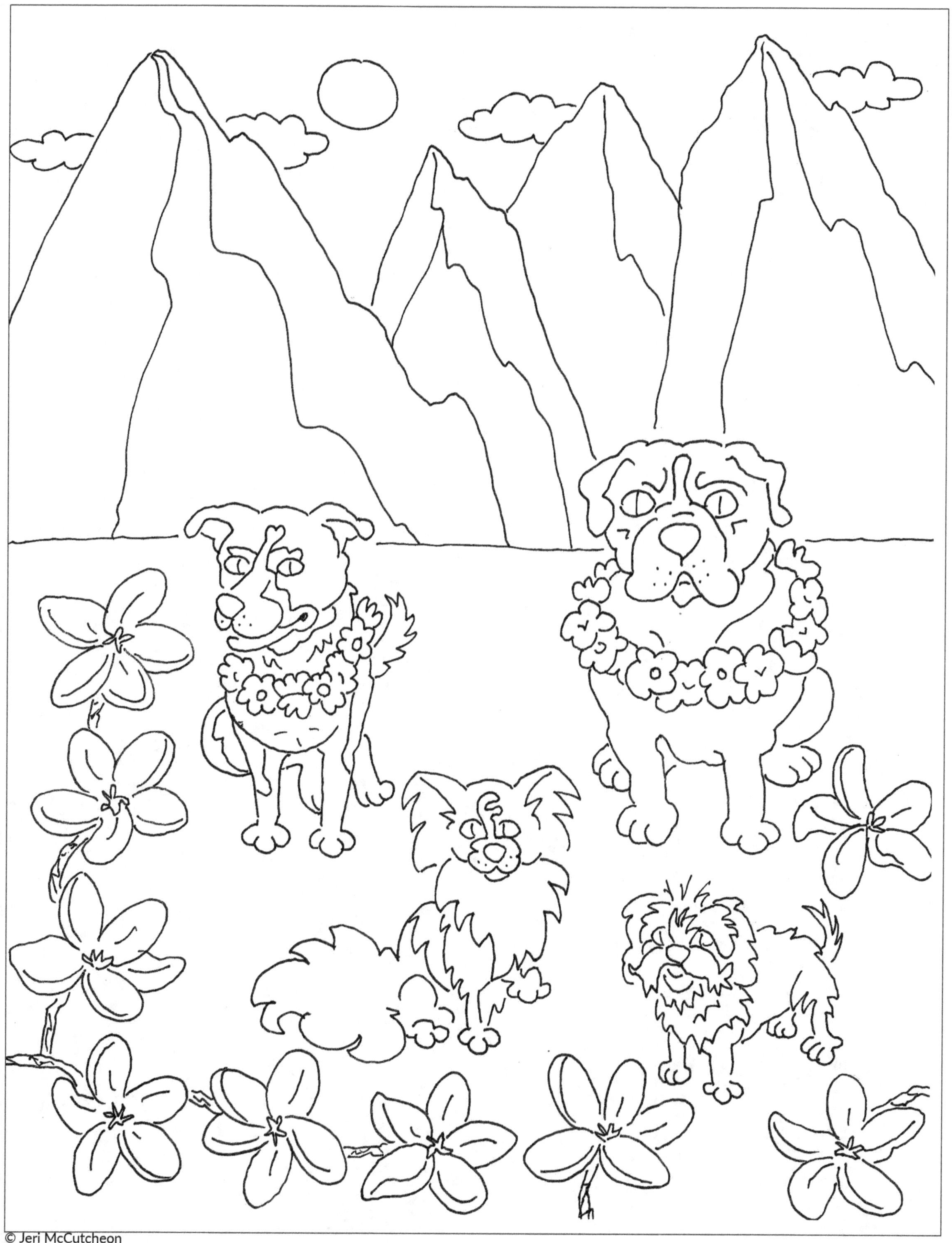

© Jeri McCutcheon

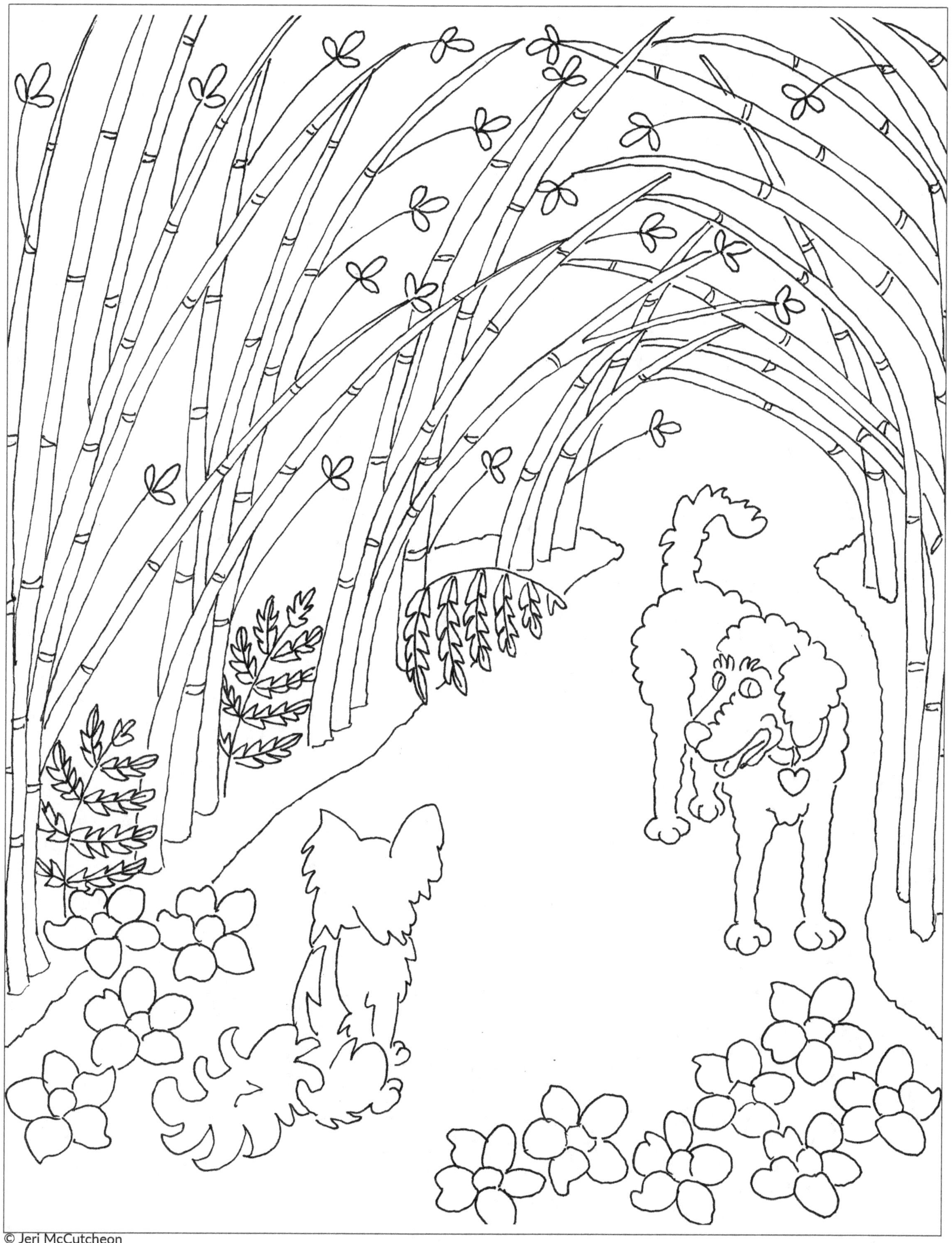

© Jeri McCutcheon

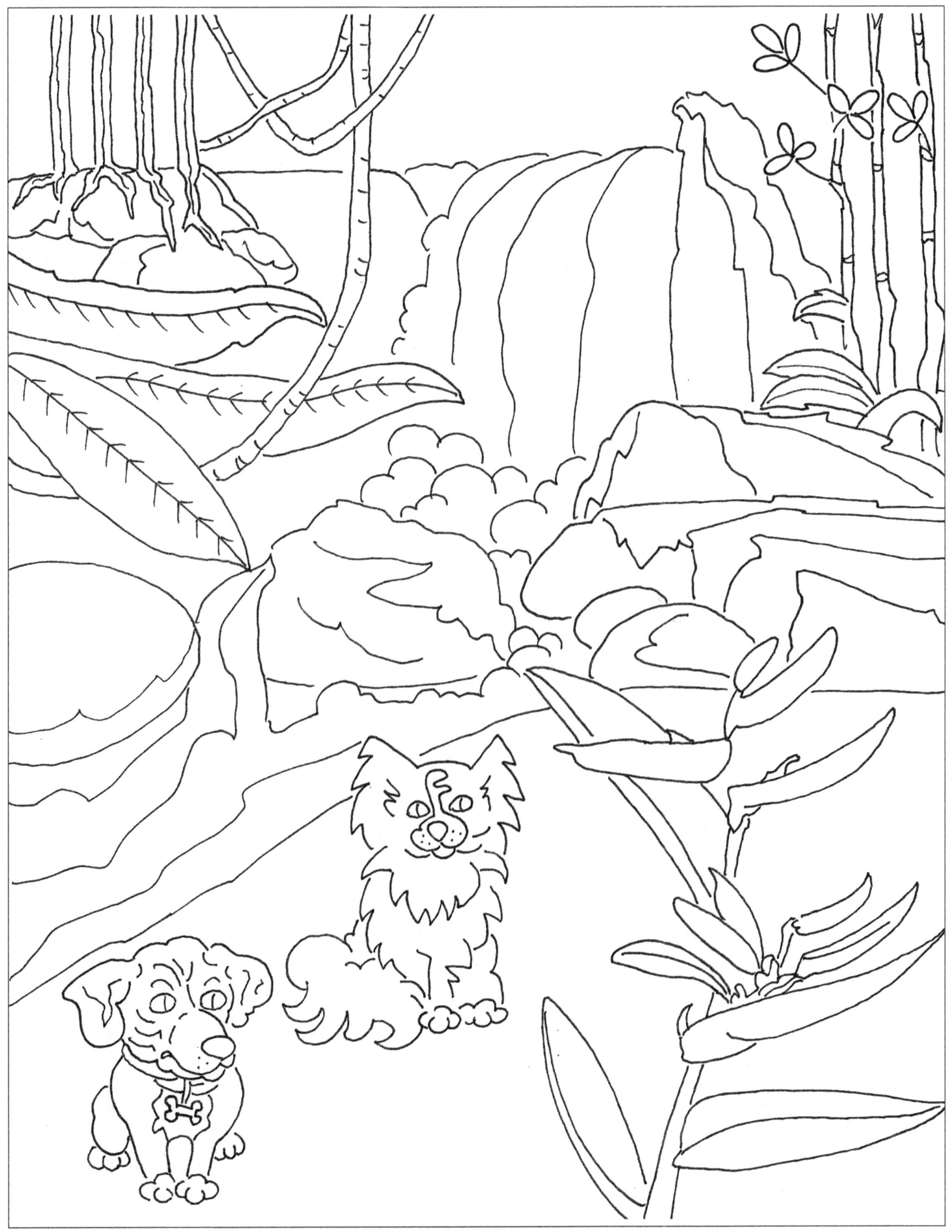

© Jeri McCutcheon

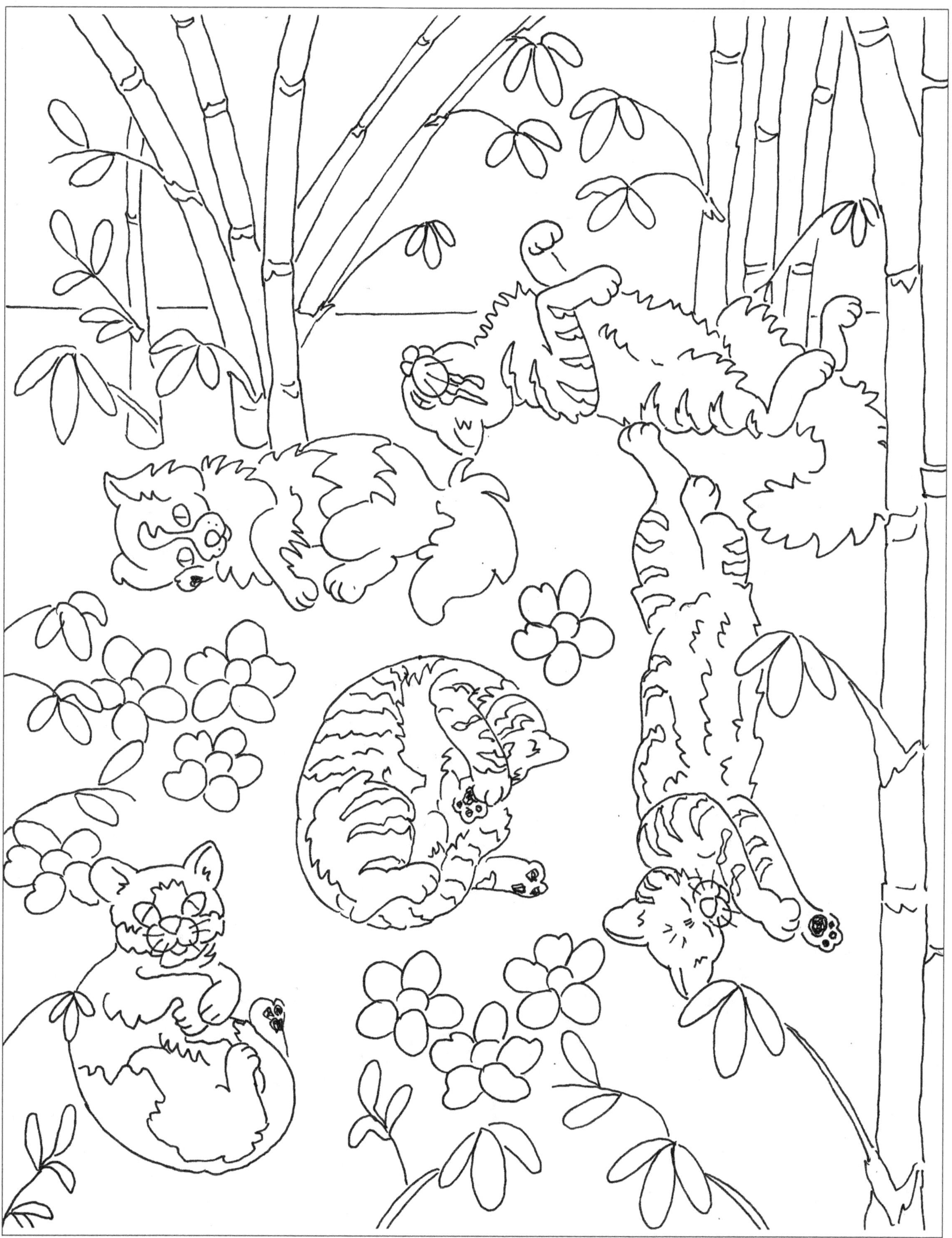

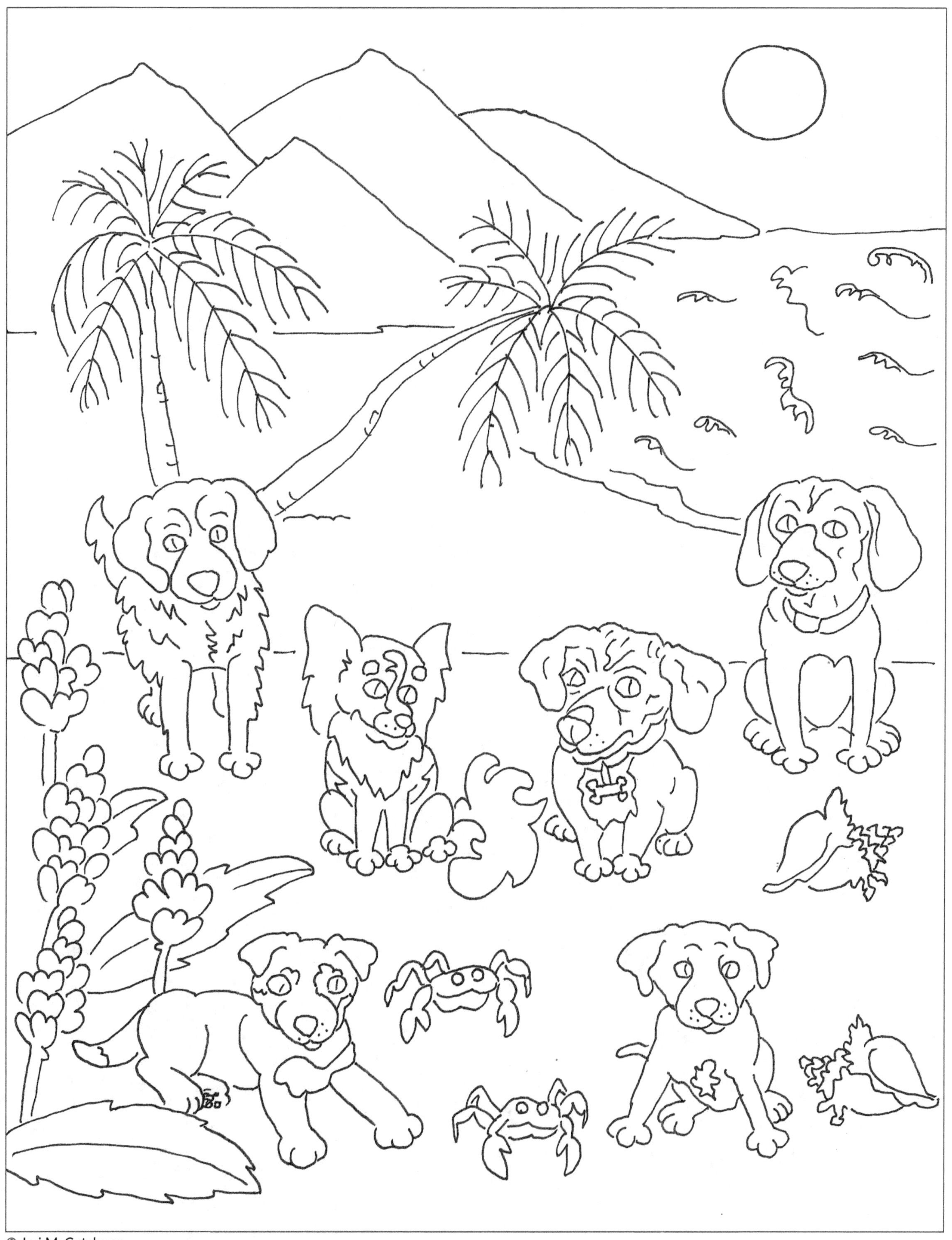

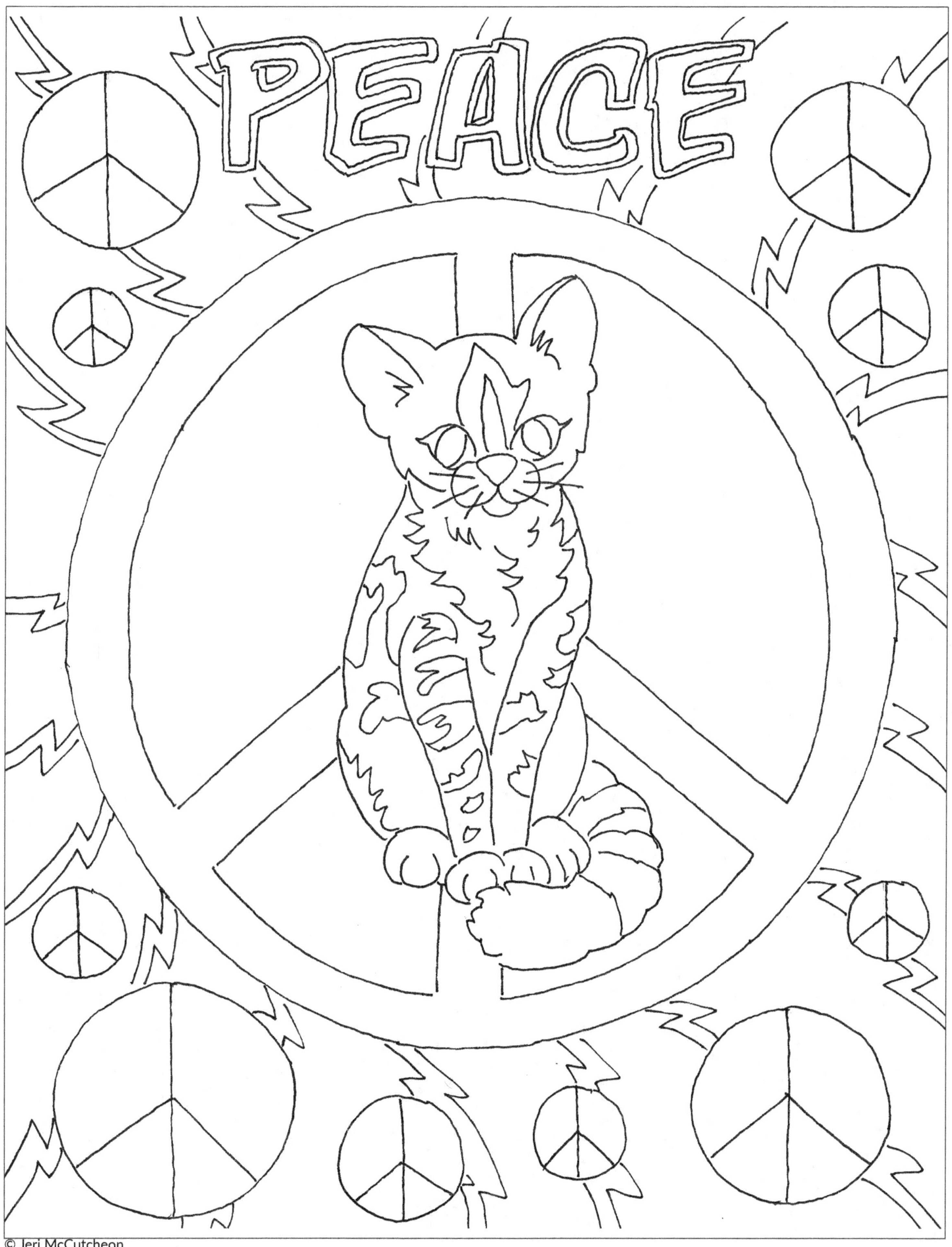

© Jeri McCutcheon

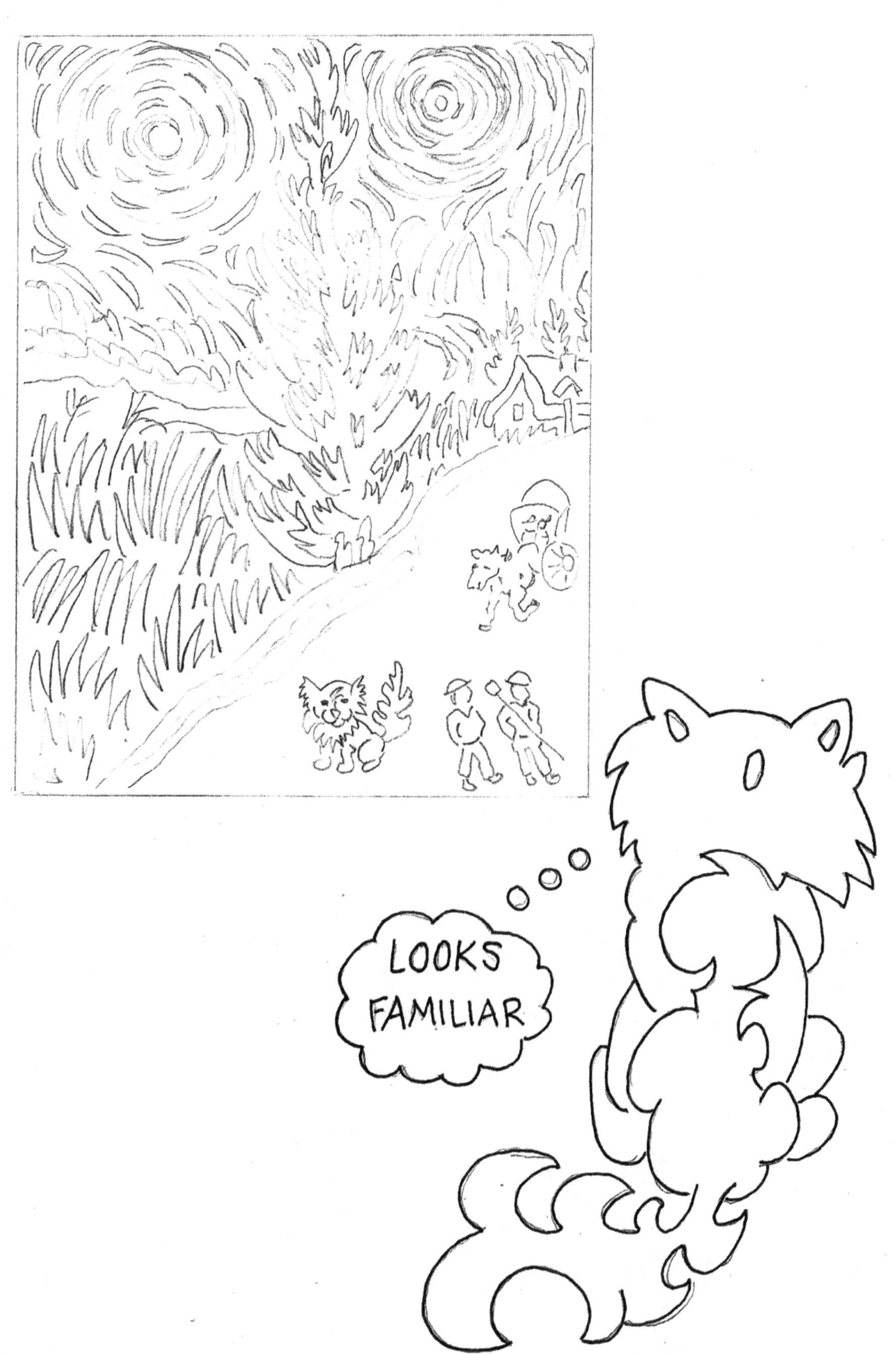

© Jeri McCutcheon

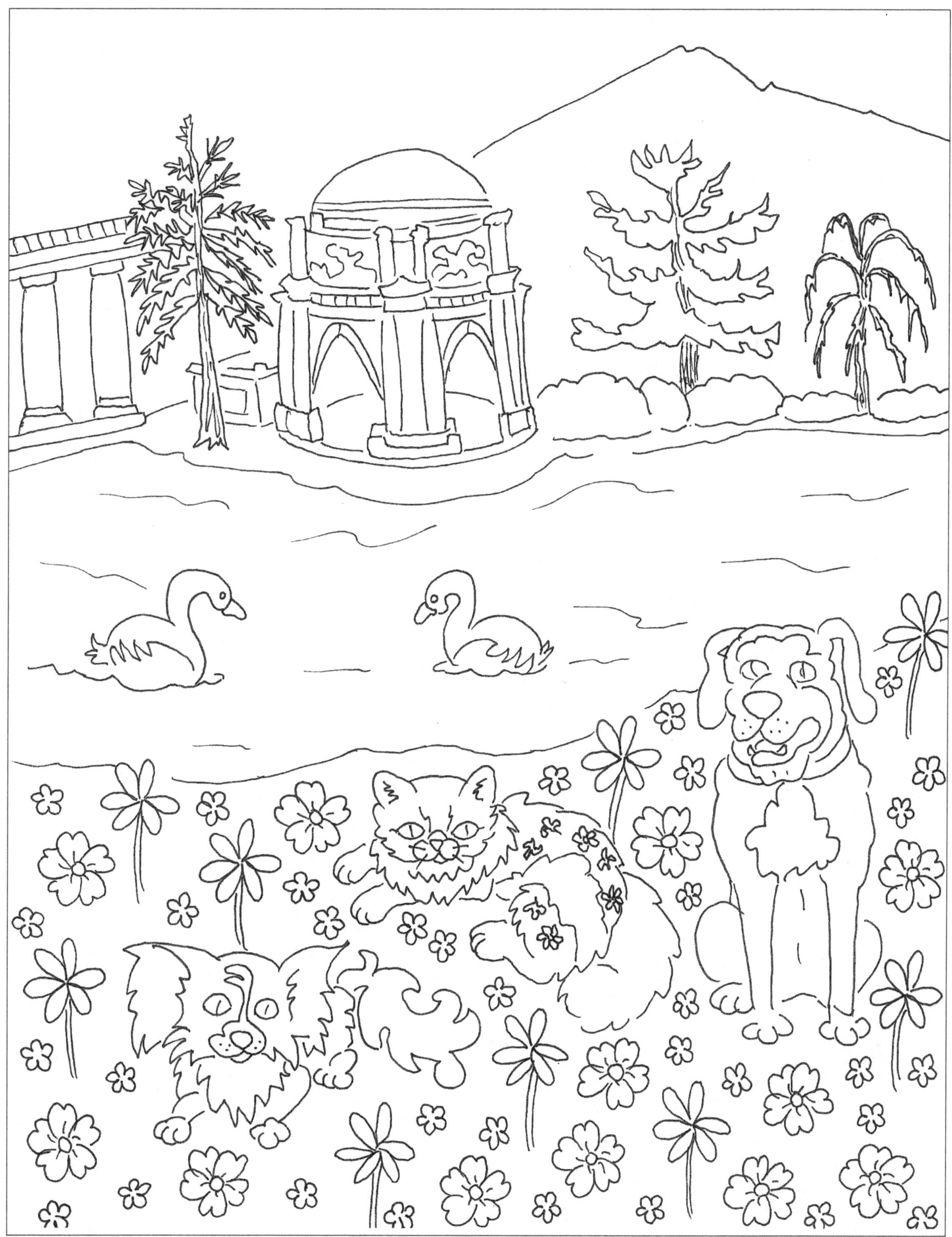

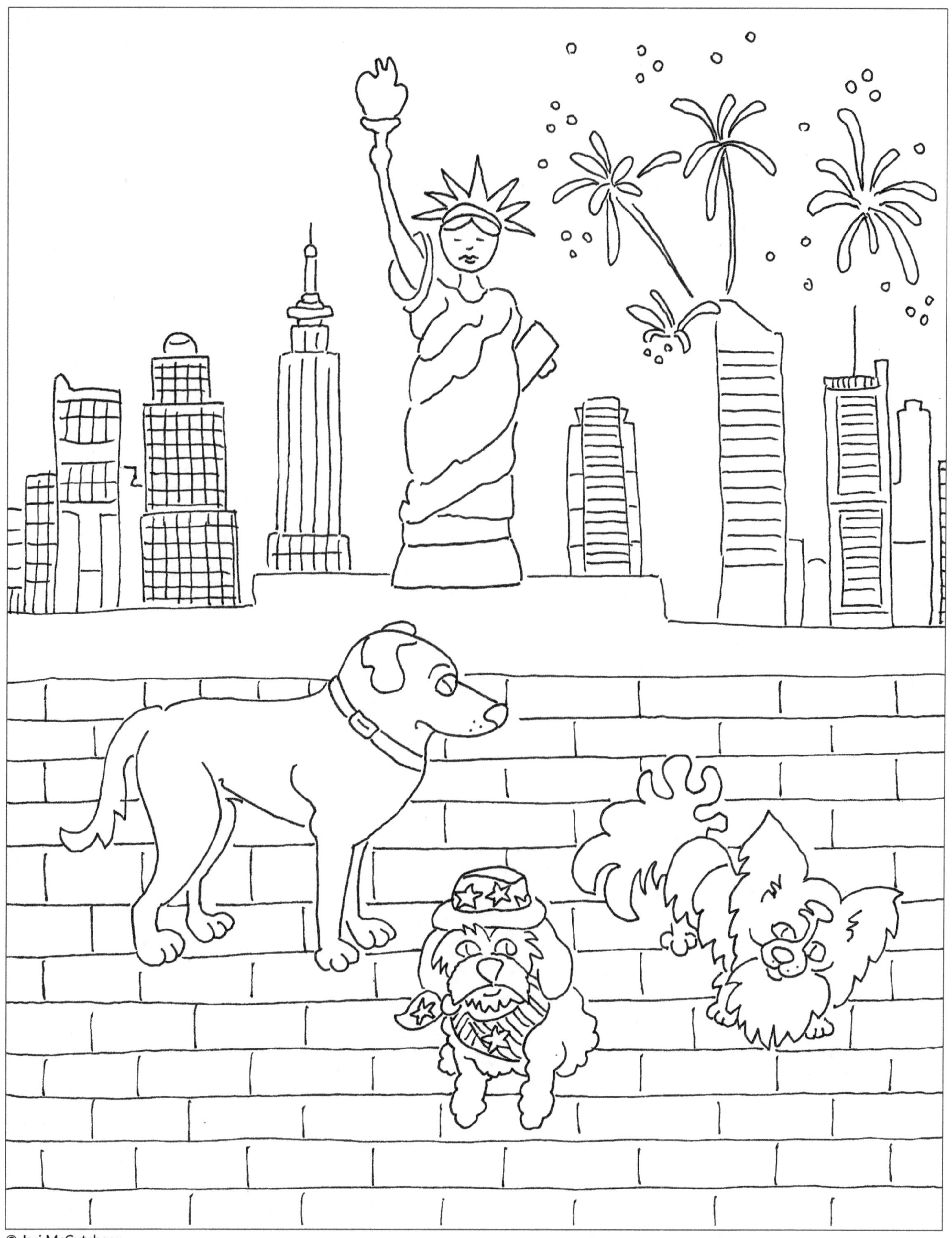

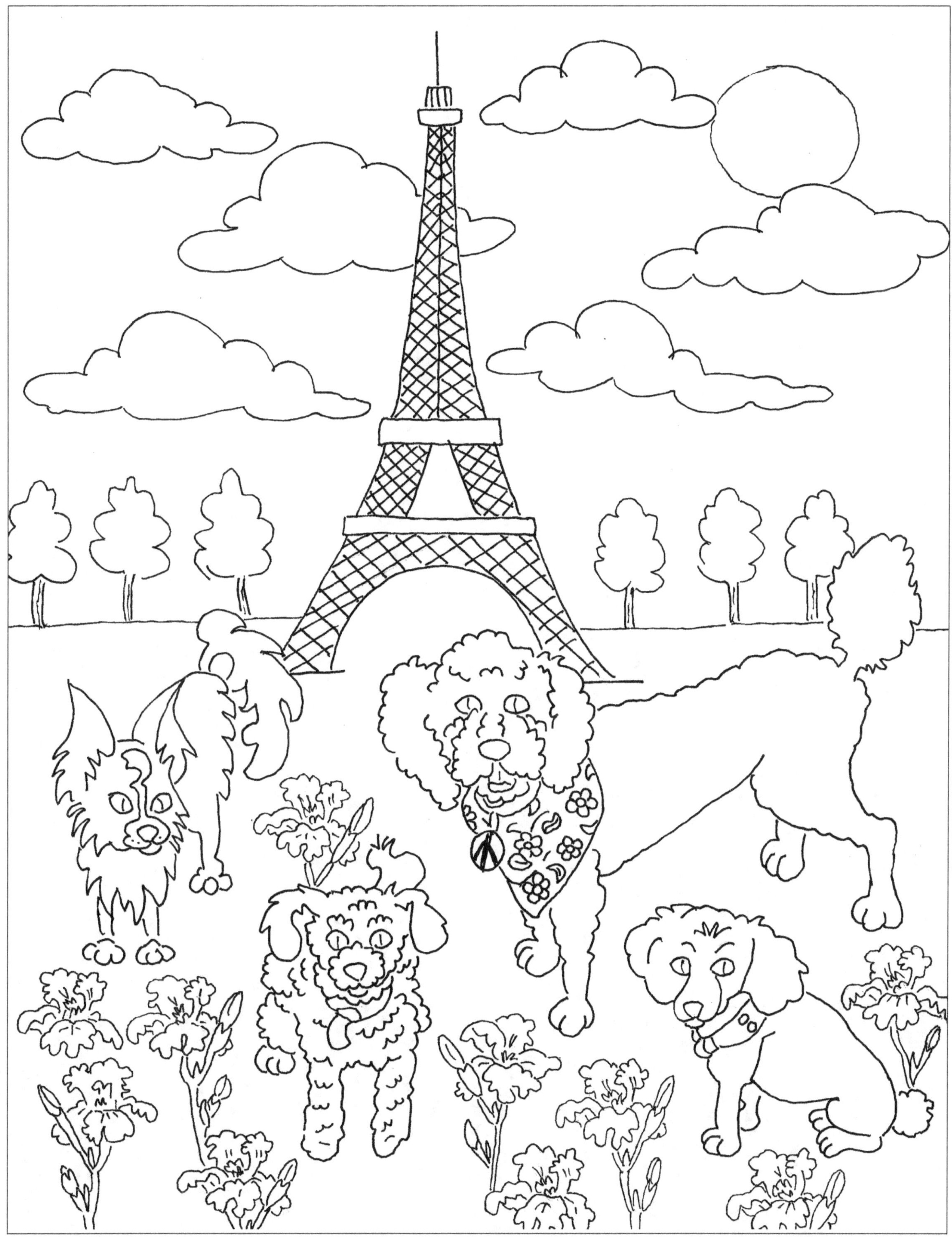

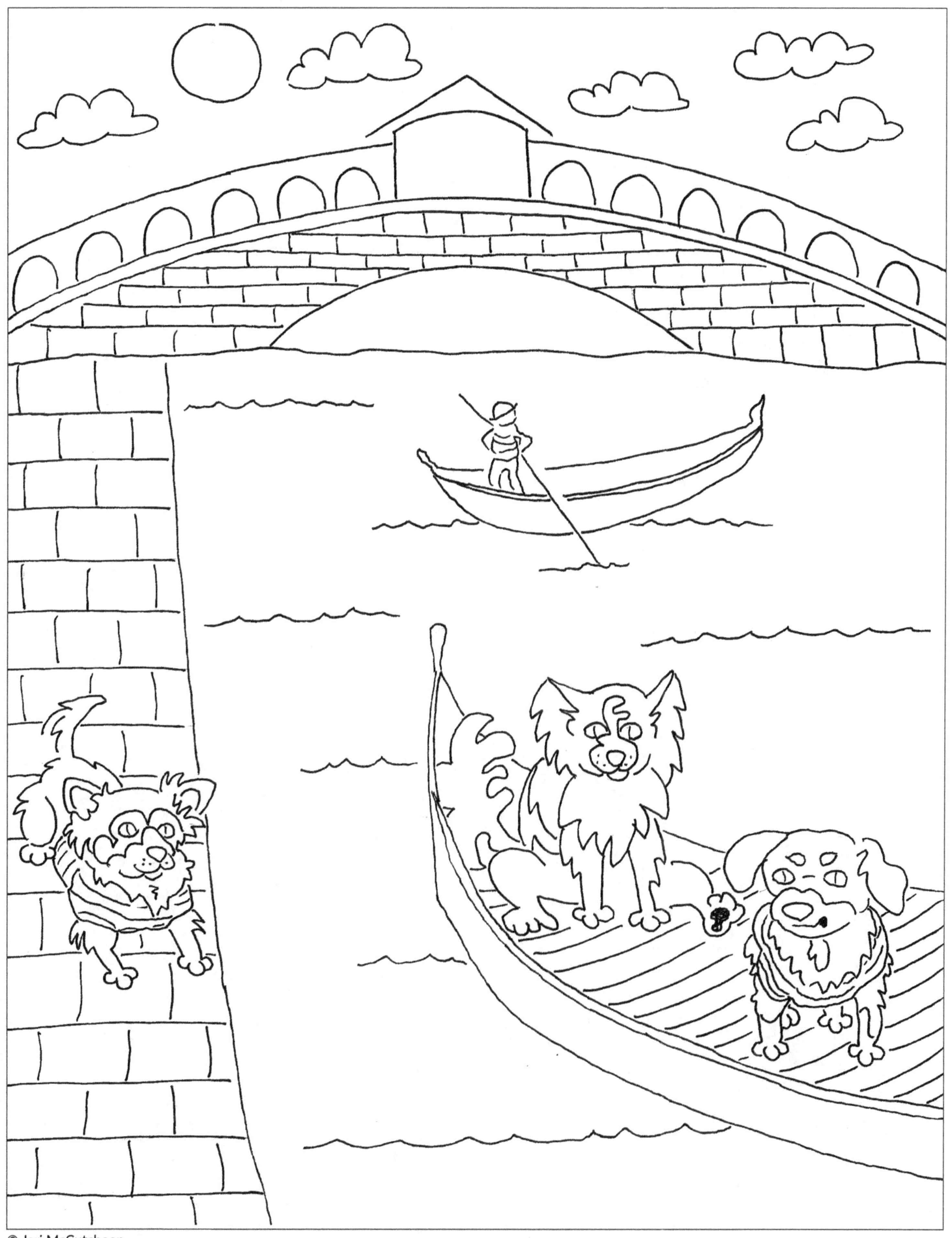

© Jeri McCutcheon

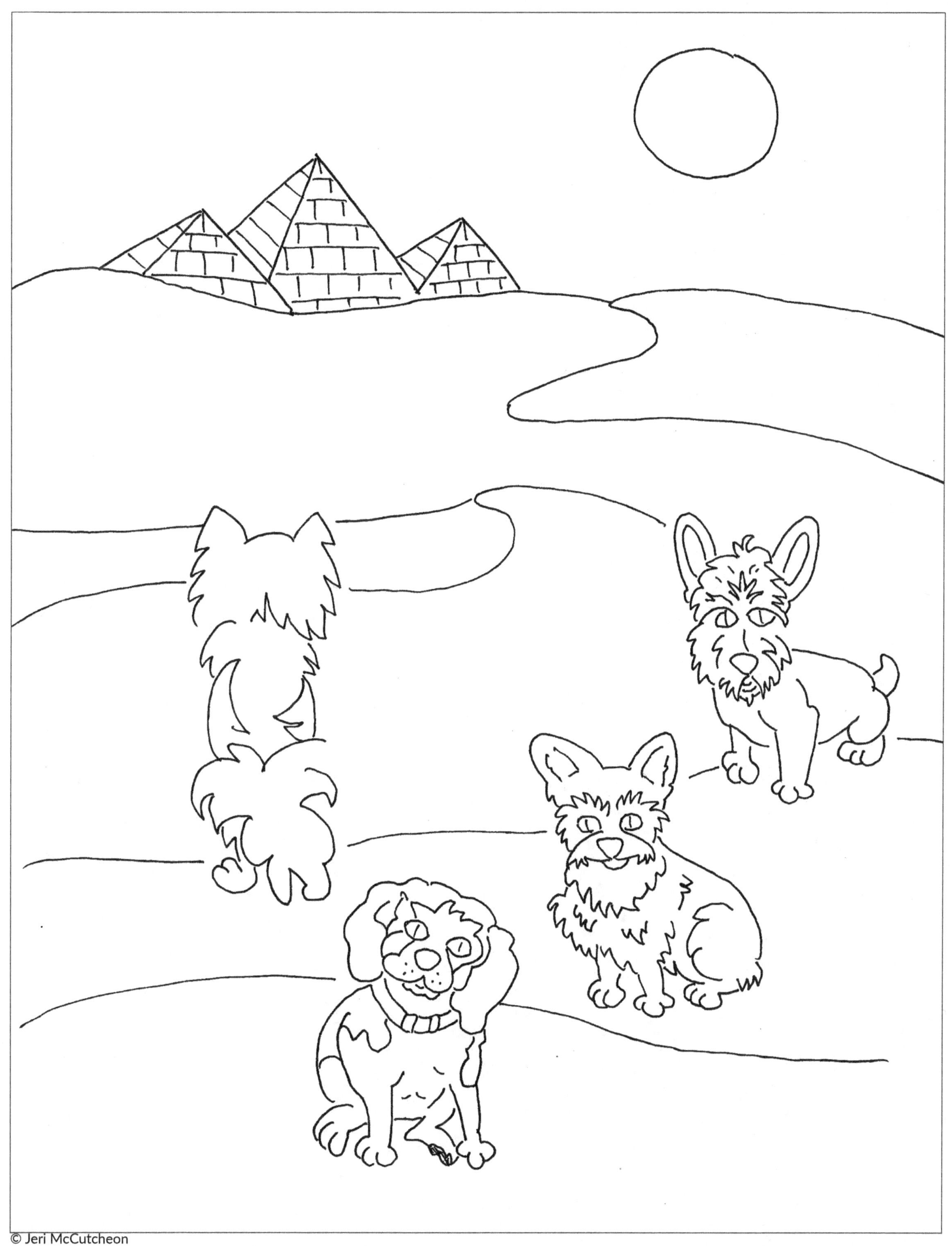

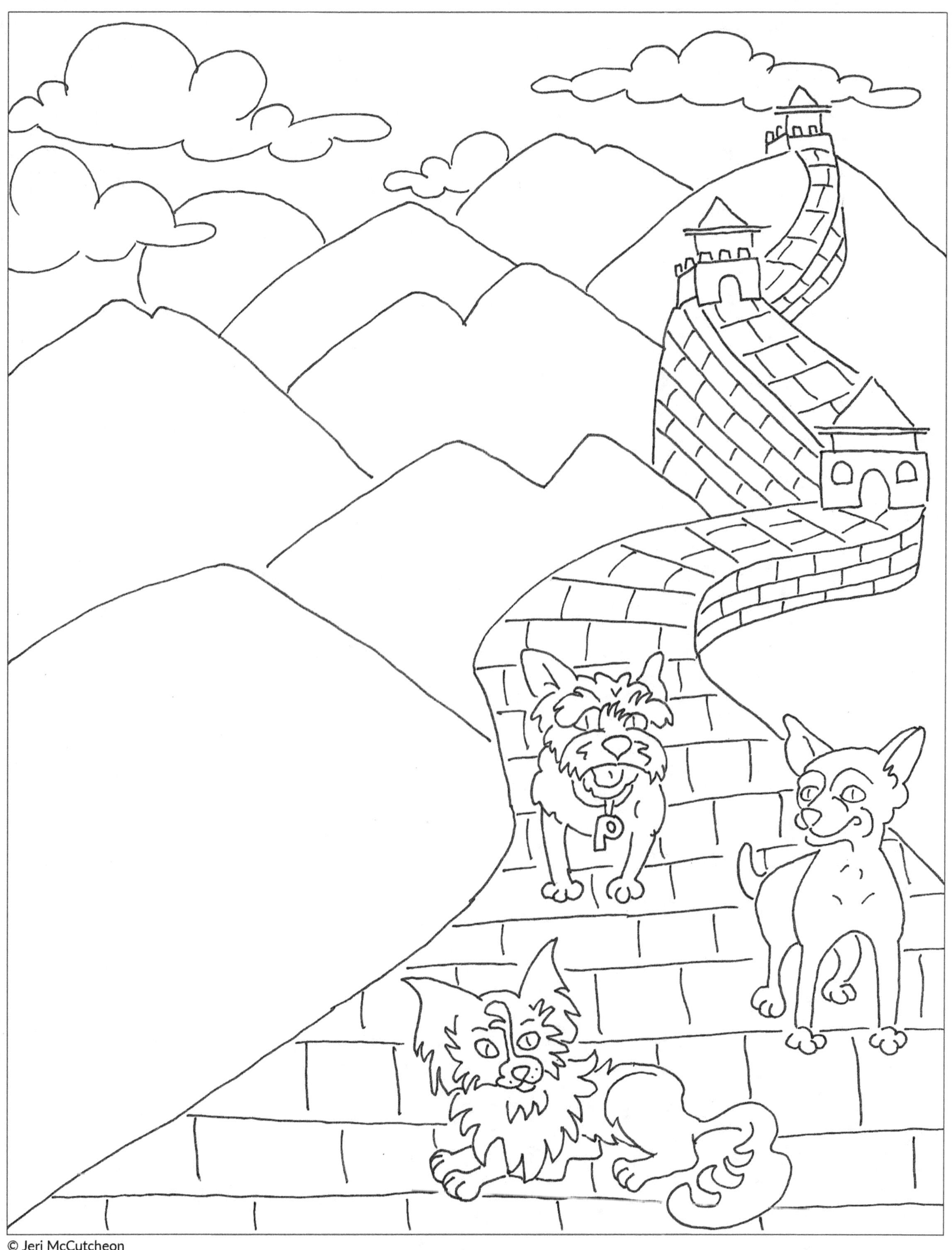

© Jeri McCutcheon

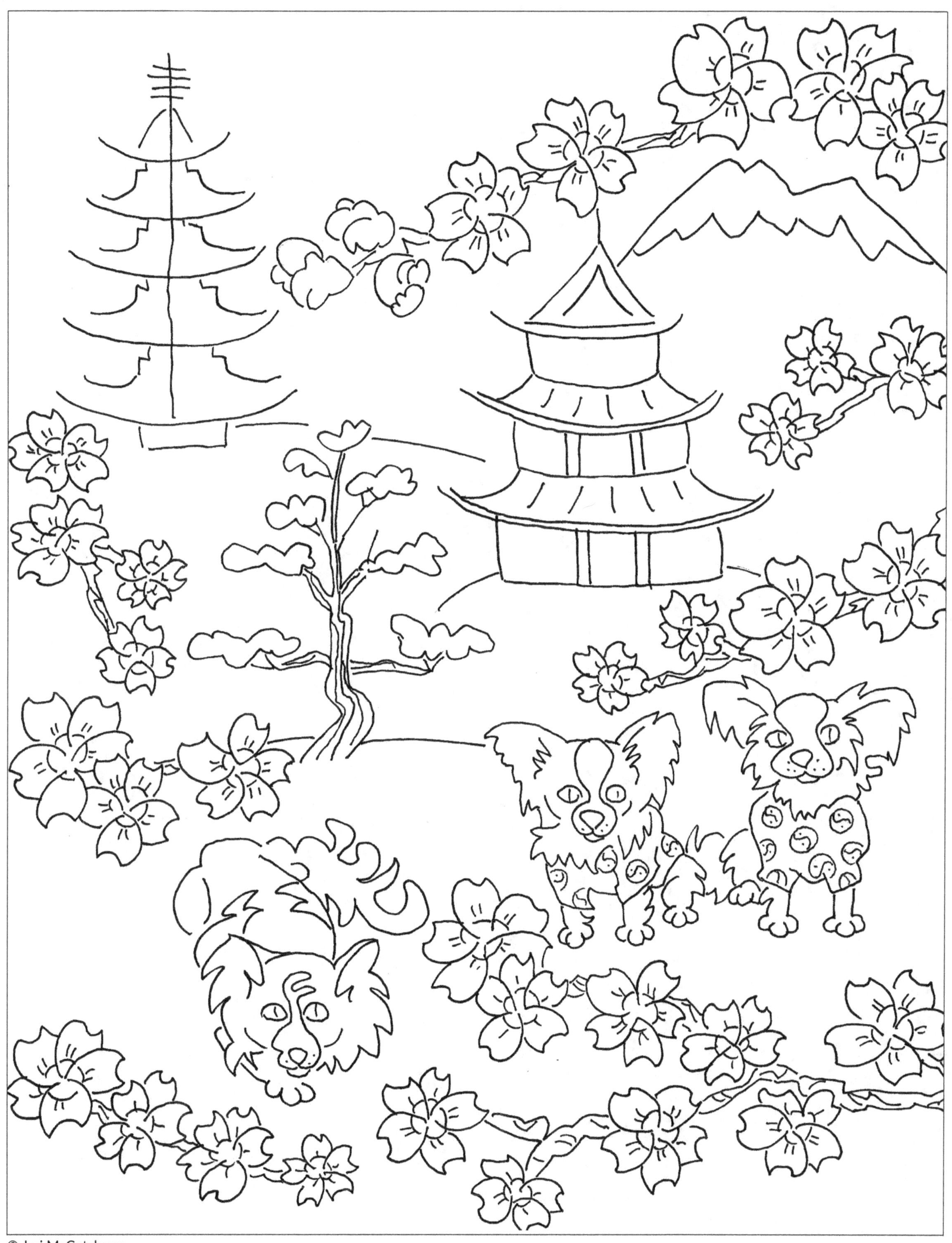

© Jeri McCutcheon

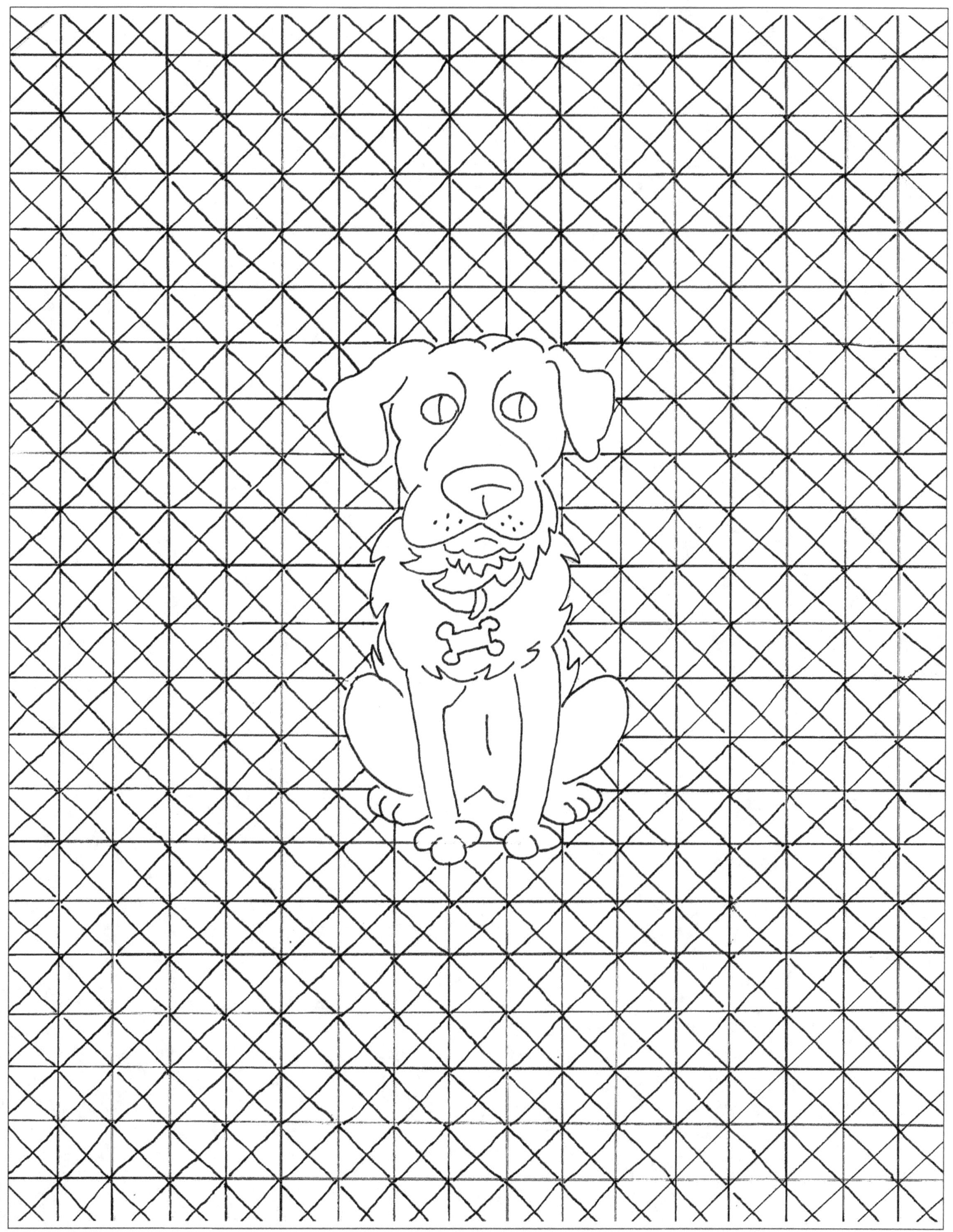

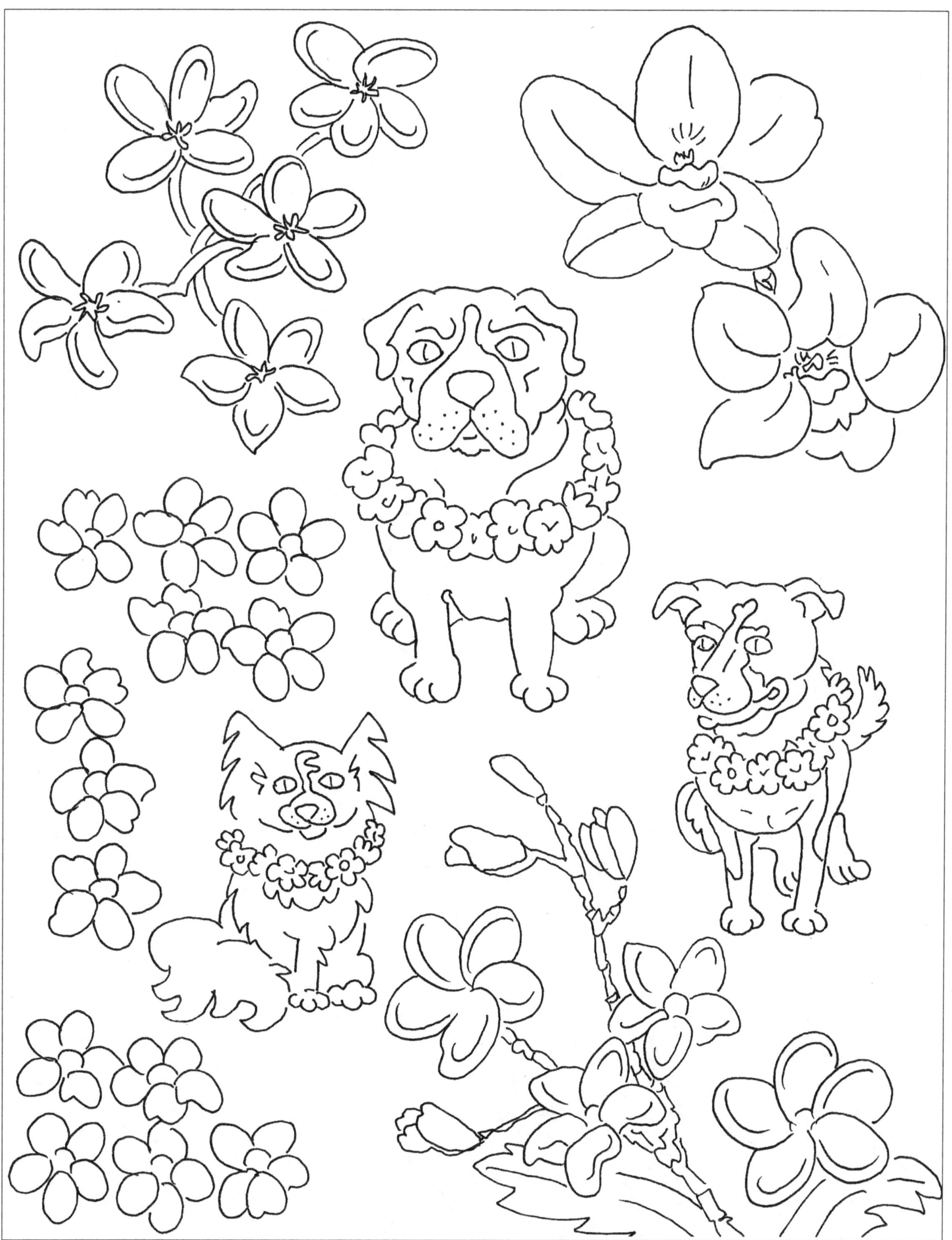

SO LONG FOR NOW

FROM WAGGLE TAIL

COLORING IS FUN

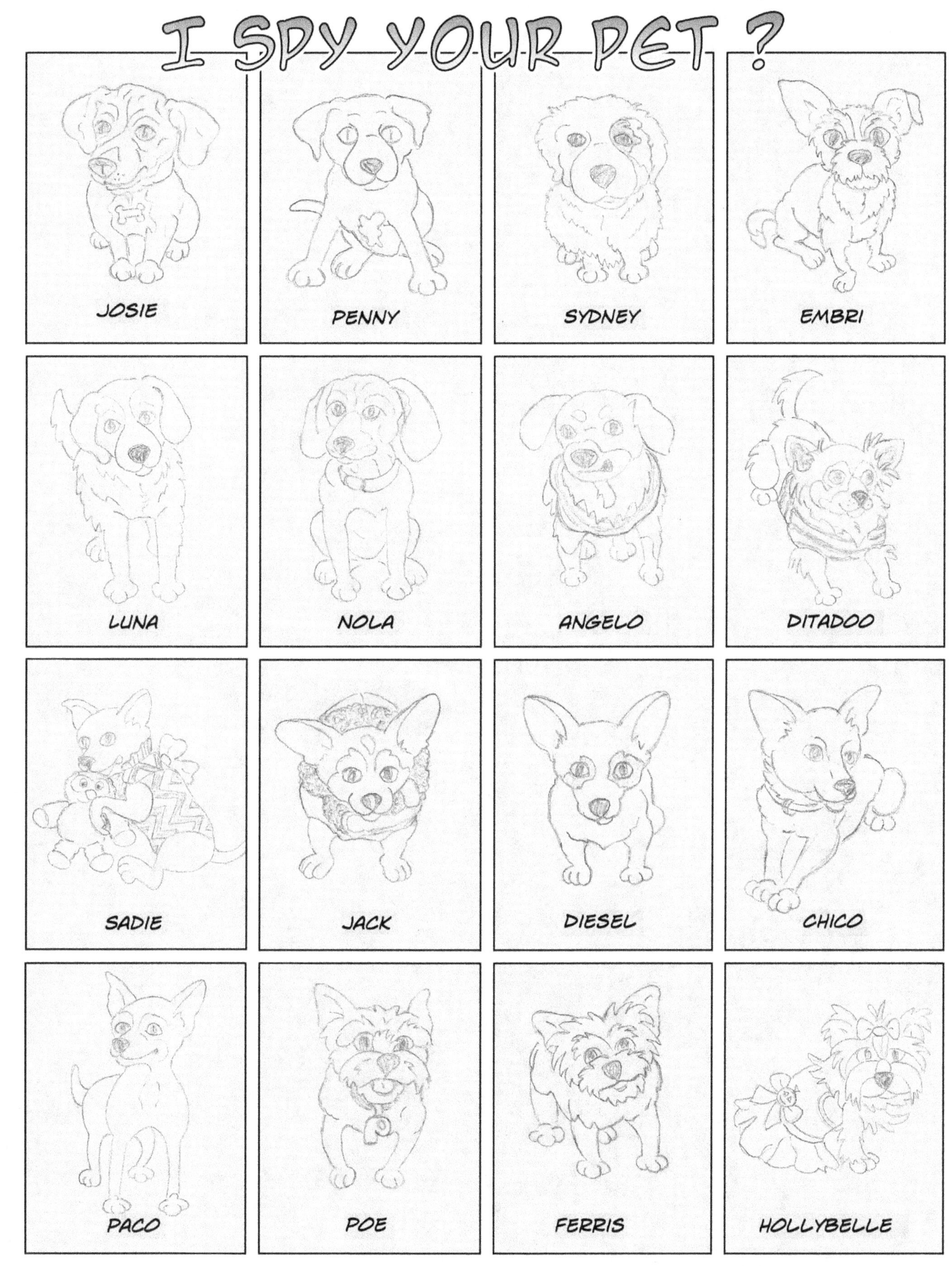

I SPY YOUR PET ?
JOSIE
PENNY
SYDNEY
EMBRI
LUNA
NOLA
ANGELO
DITADOO
SADIE
JACK
DIESEL
CHICO
PACO
POE
FERRIS
HOLLYBELLE

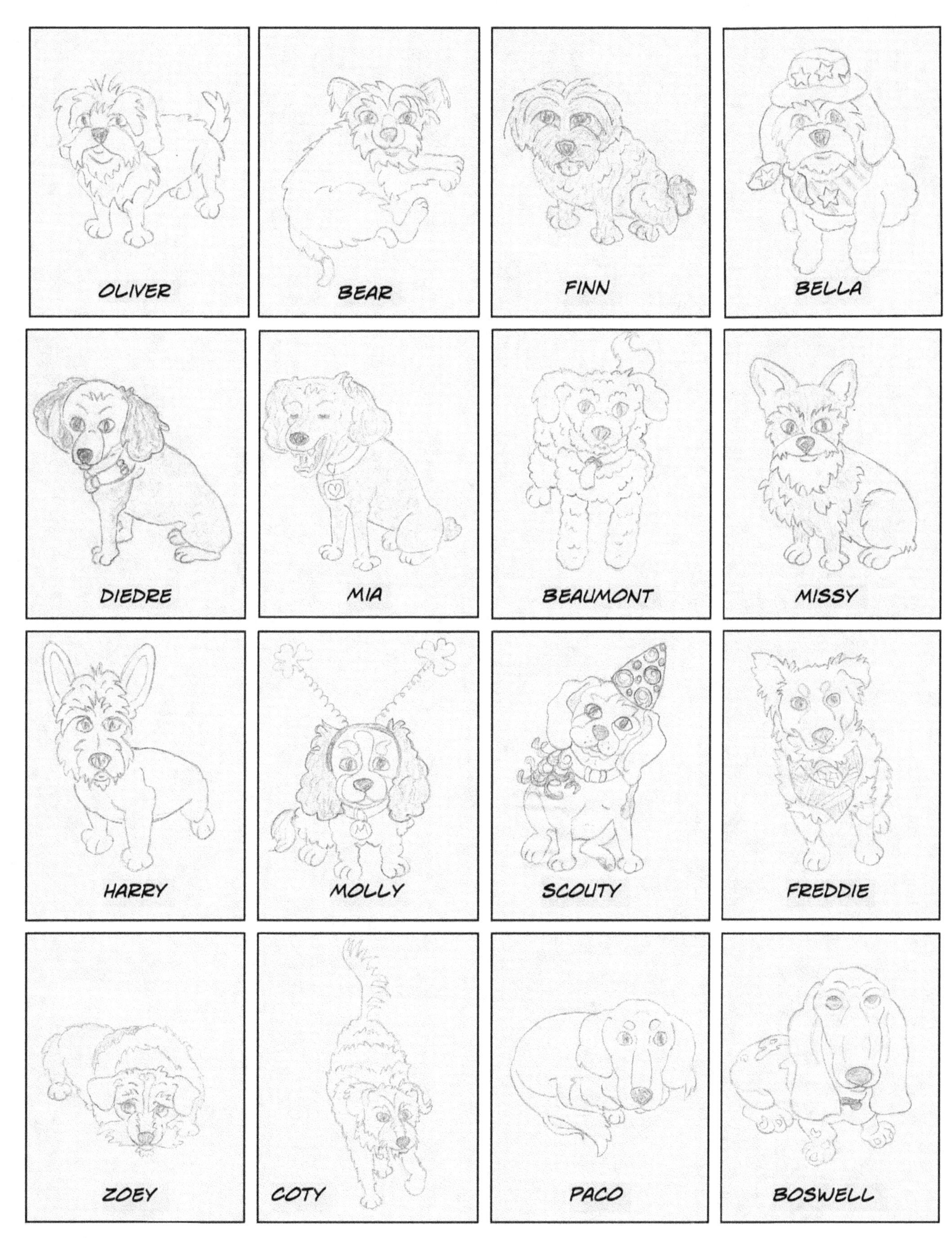

OLIVER
BEAR
FINN
BELLA
DIEDRE
MIA
BEAUMONT
MISSY
HARRY
MOLLY
SCOUTY
FREDDIE
ZOEY
COTY
PACO
BOSWELL

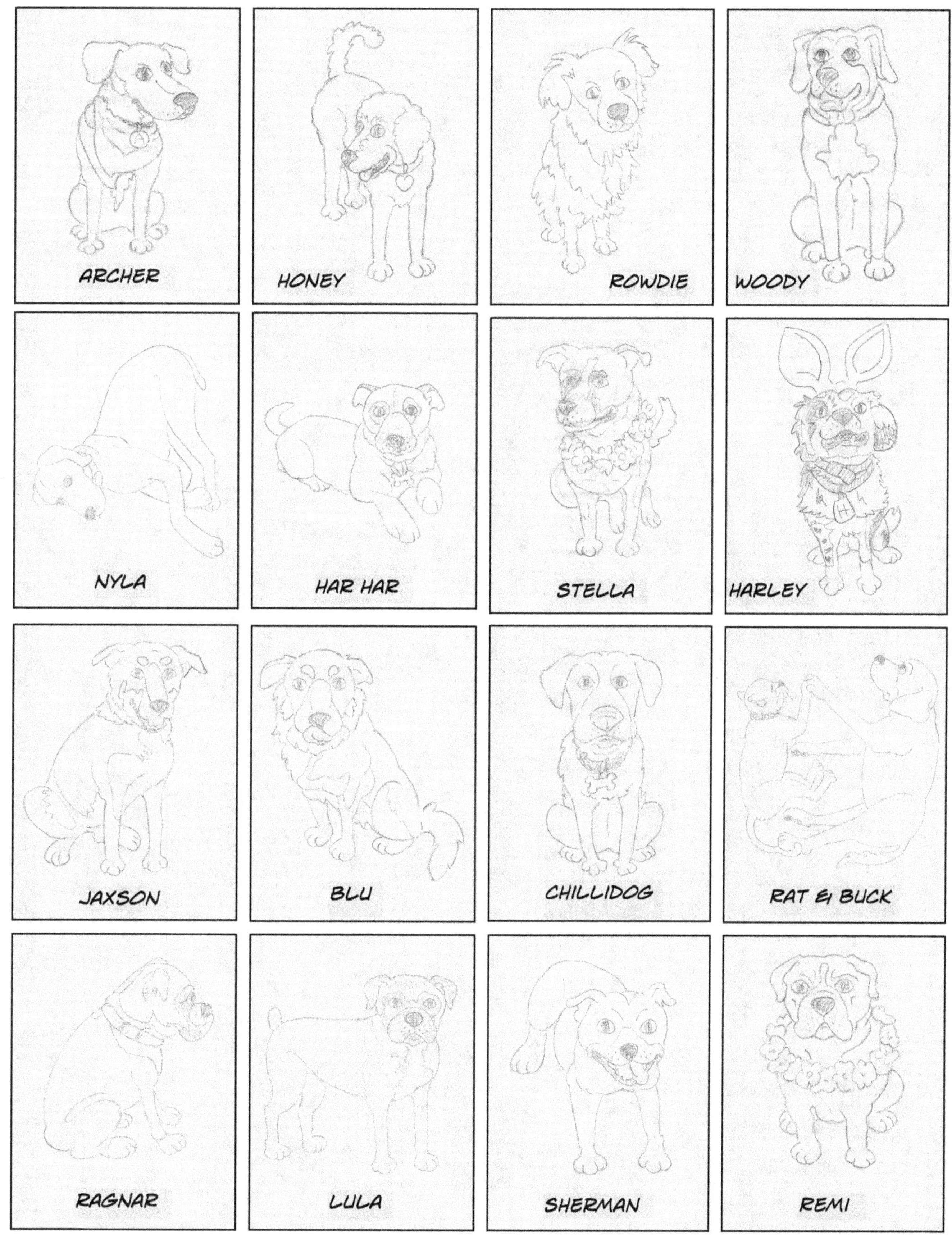

ARCHER
HONEY
ROWDIE
WOODY
NYLA
HAR HAR
STELLA
HARLEY
JAXSON
BLU
CHILLIDOG
RAT & BUCK
RAGNAR
LULA
SHERMAN
REMI

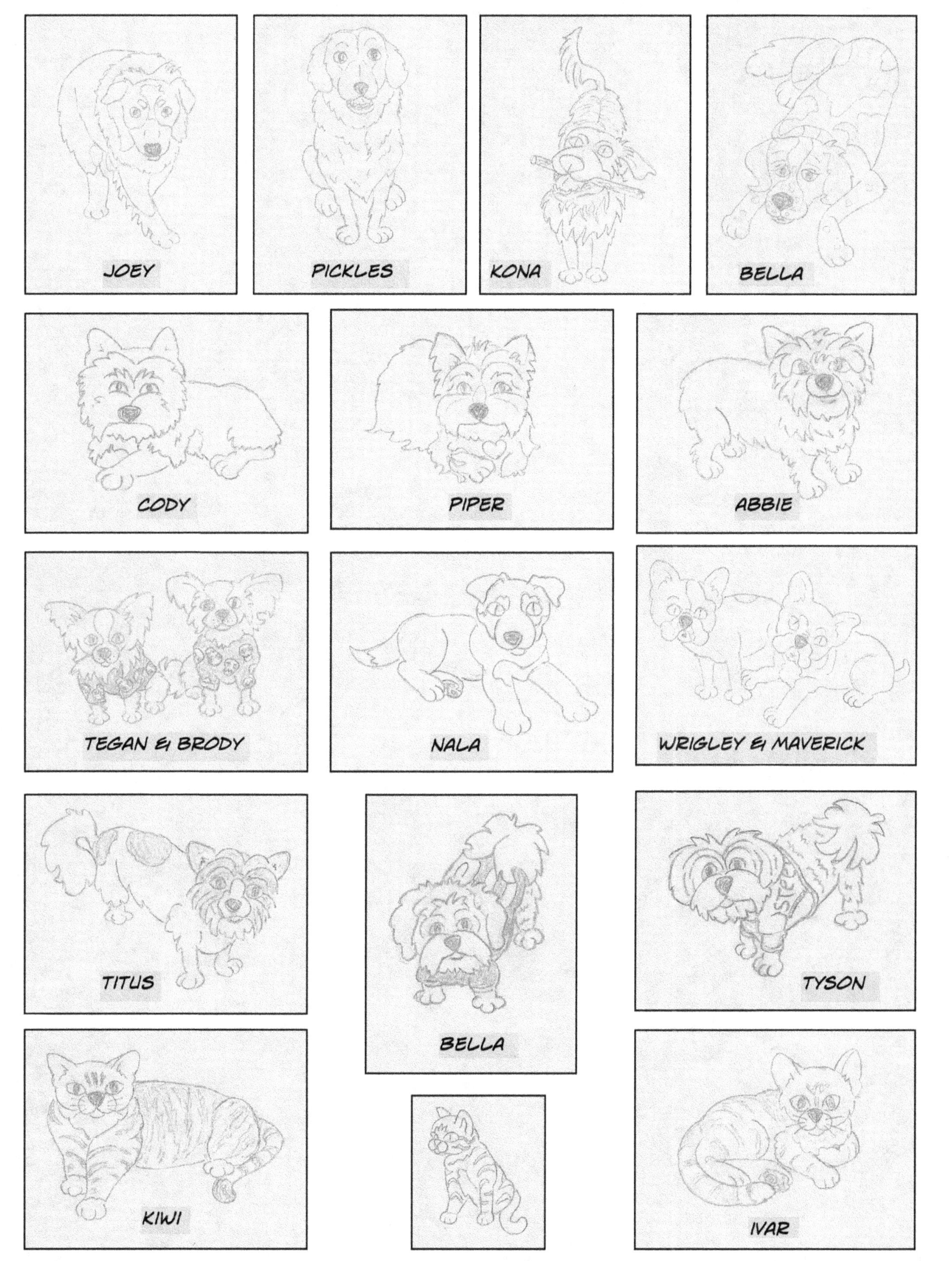

JOEY
PICKLES
KONA
BELLA
CODY
PIPER
ABBIE
TEGAN & BRODY
NALA
WRIGLEY & MAVERICK
TITUS
BELLA
TYSON
KIWI
IVAR

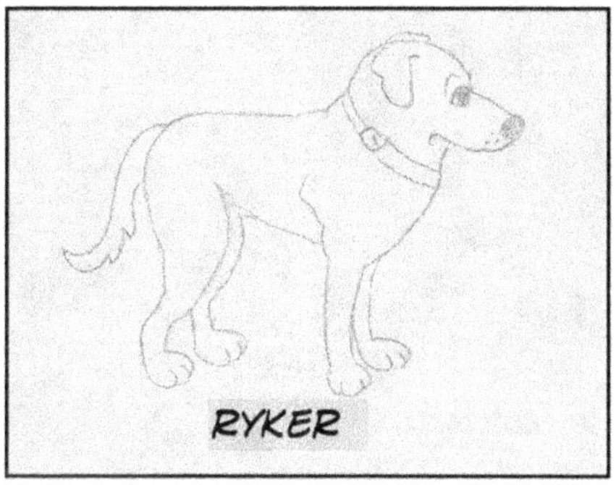

RYKER	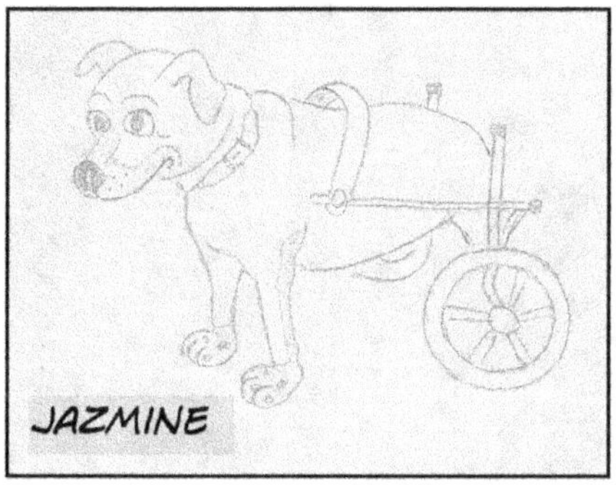 JAZMINE	SPENCER
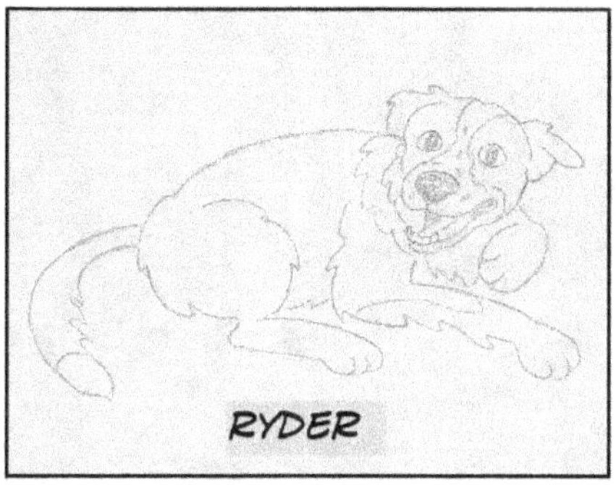 RYDER	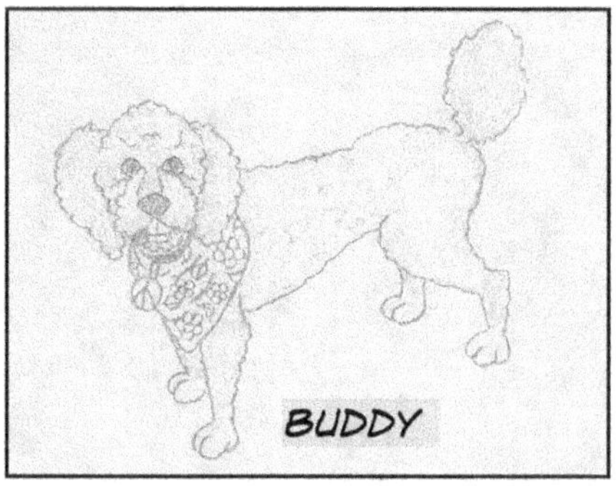 BUDDY	GRACIE
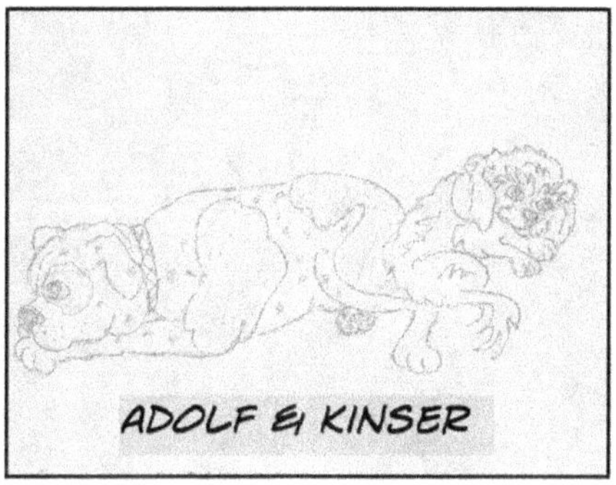 ADOLF & KINSER	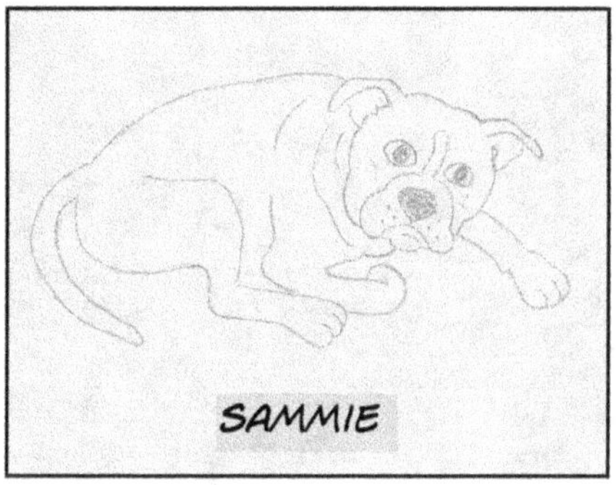 SAMMIE	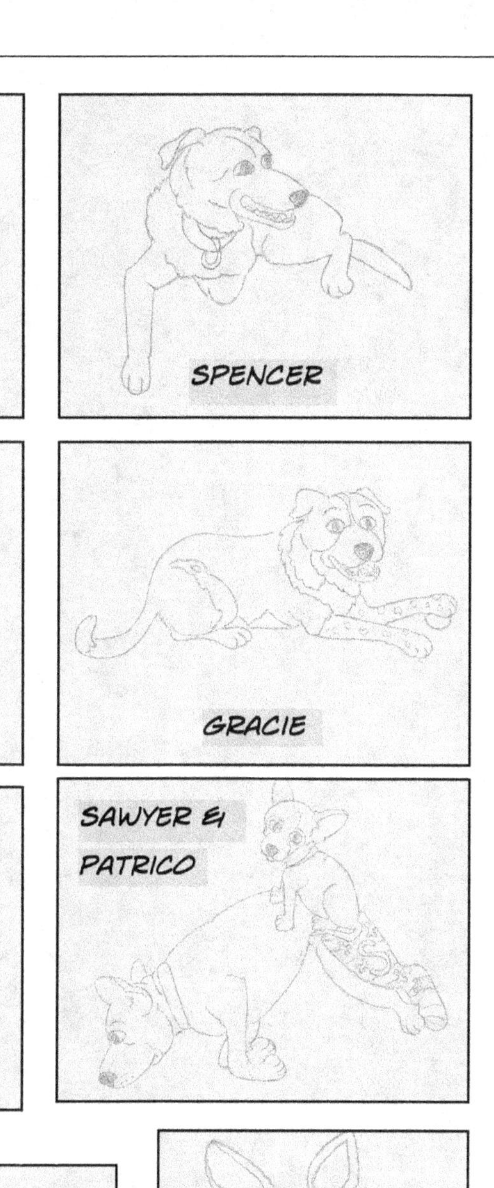SAWYER & PATRICO
HUNTER	SASHA- SKOSHI-THOR	KORA

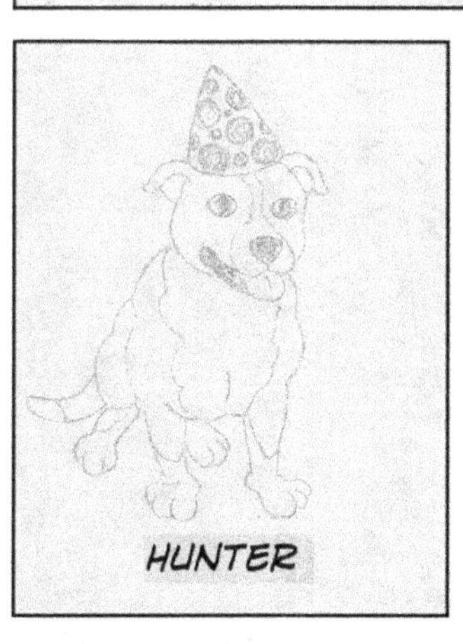RUGIE

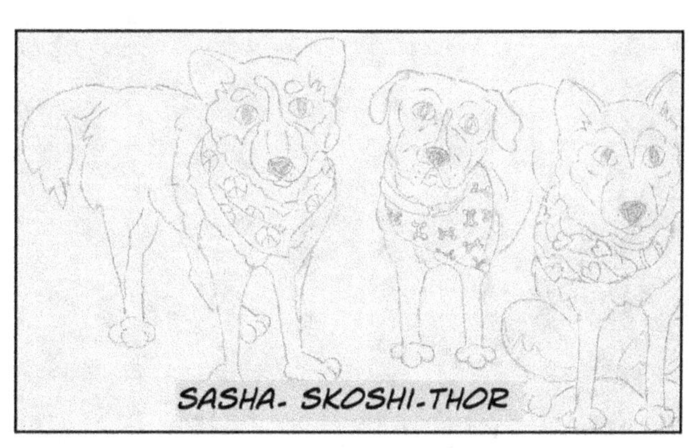

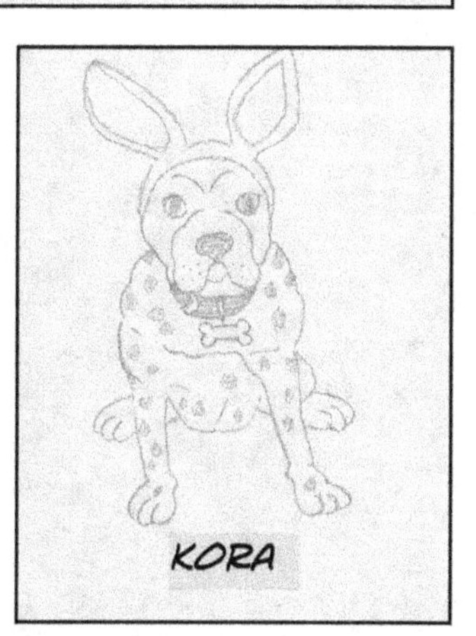

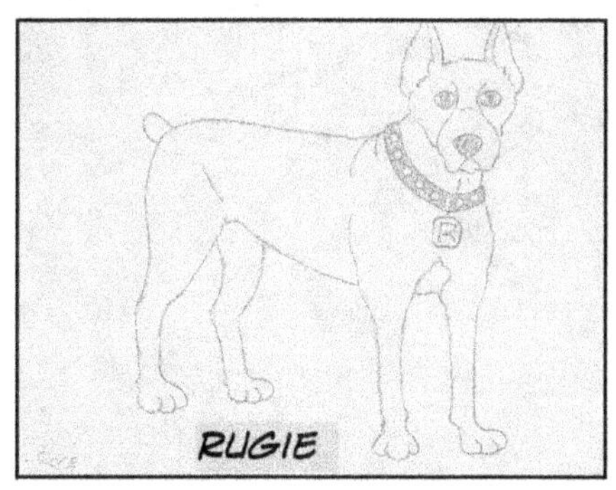RUGIE

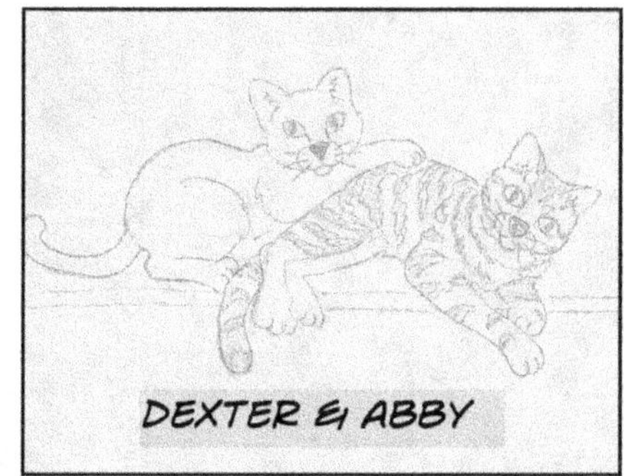DEXTER & ABBY

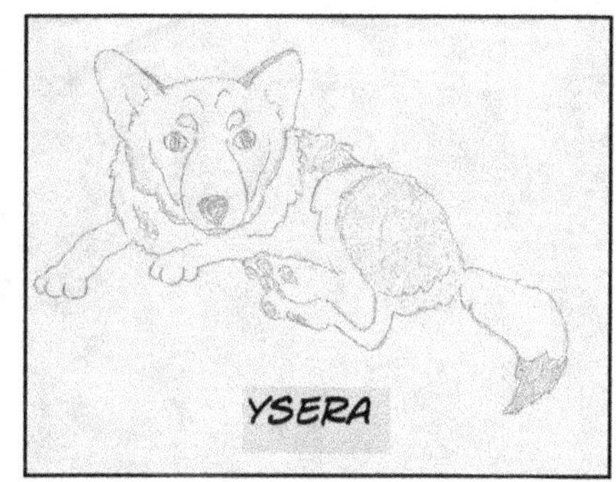YSERA

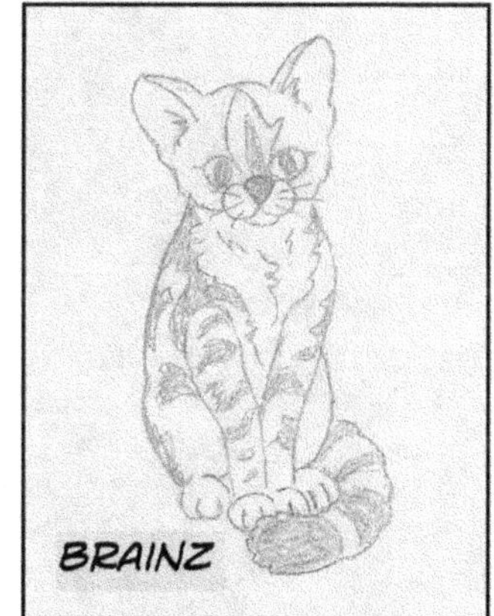

BRAINZ

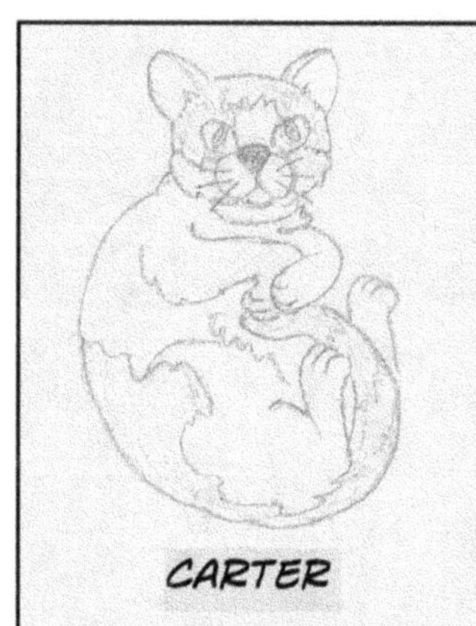

CARTER

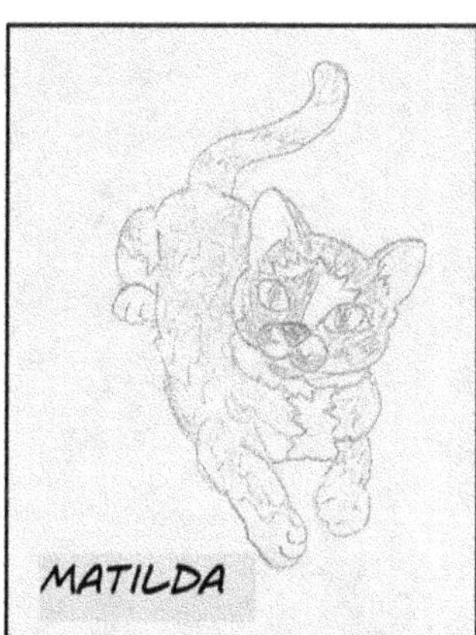

MATILDA

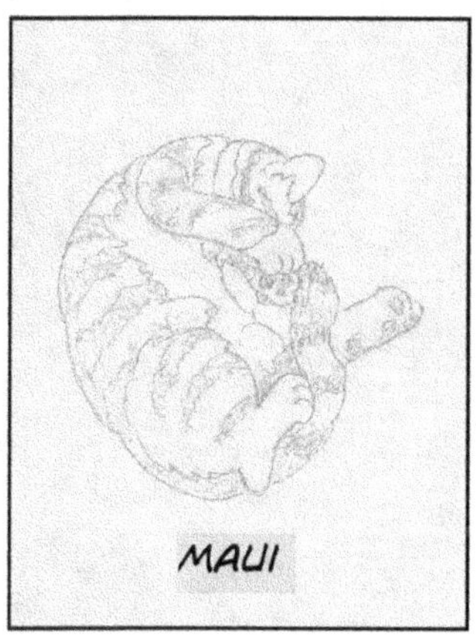

MAUI

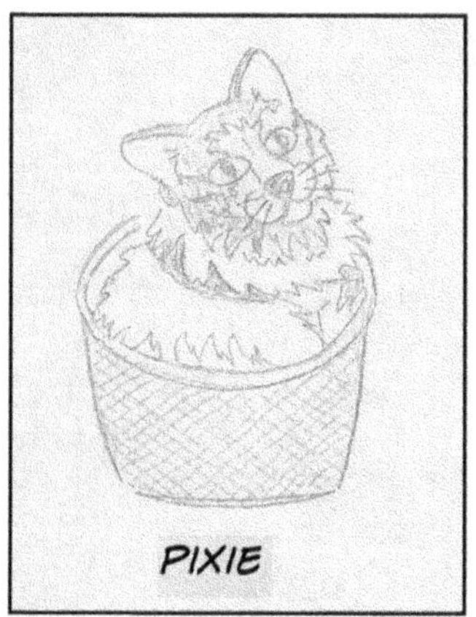

PIXIE

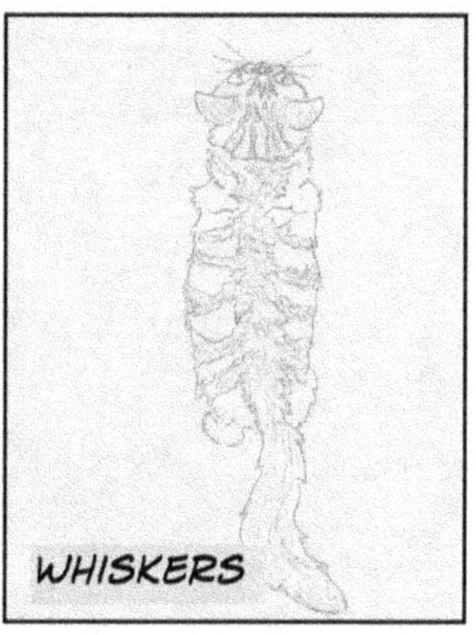

WHISKERS

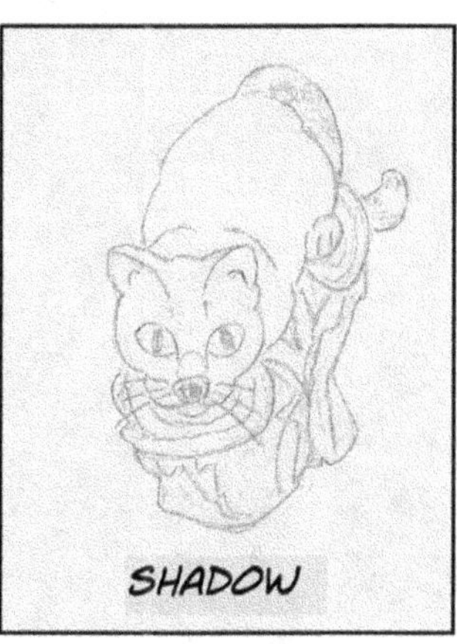

SHADOW

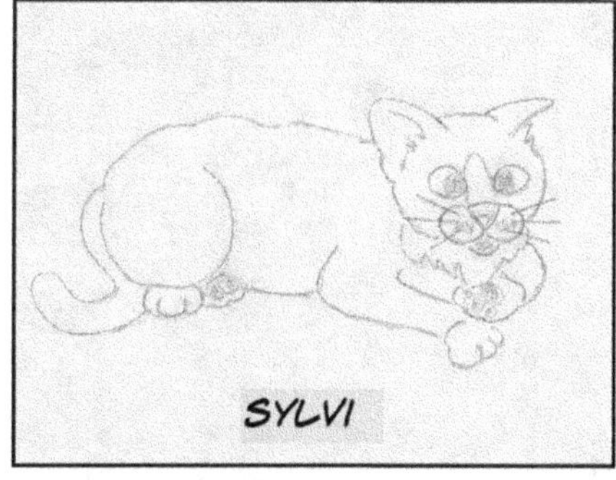

SYLVI

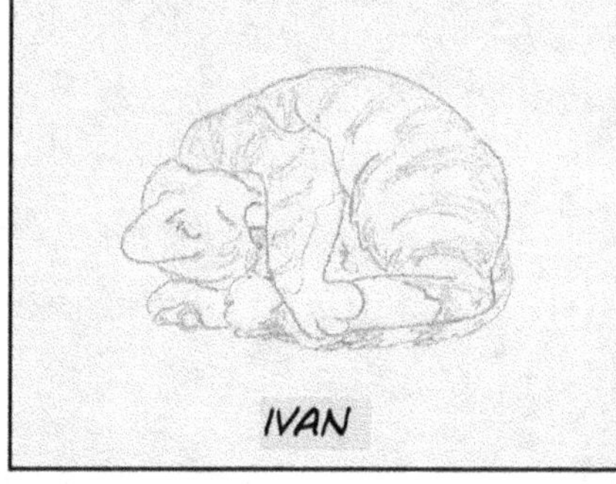

IVAN

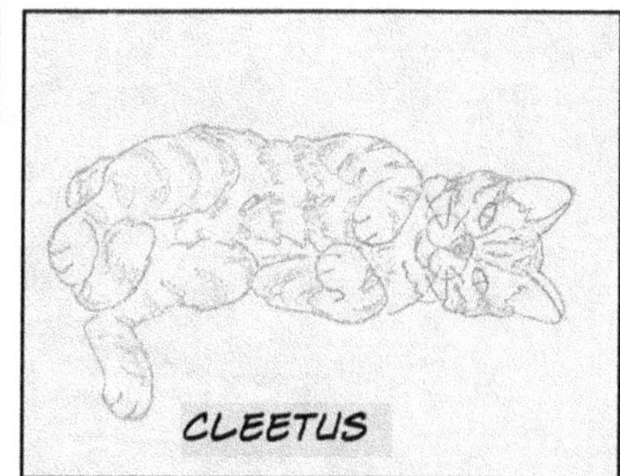

CLEETUS

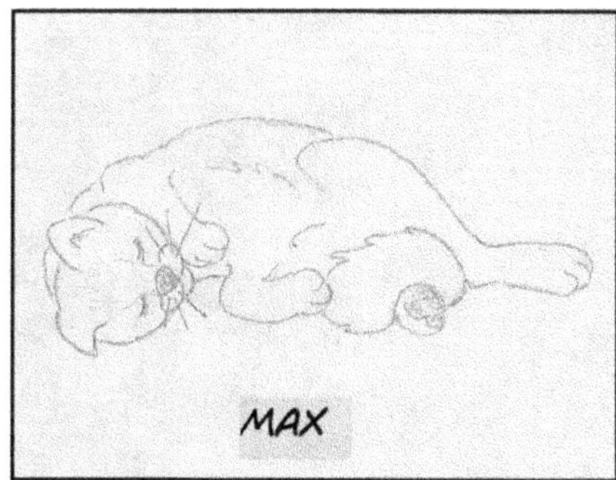

MAX

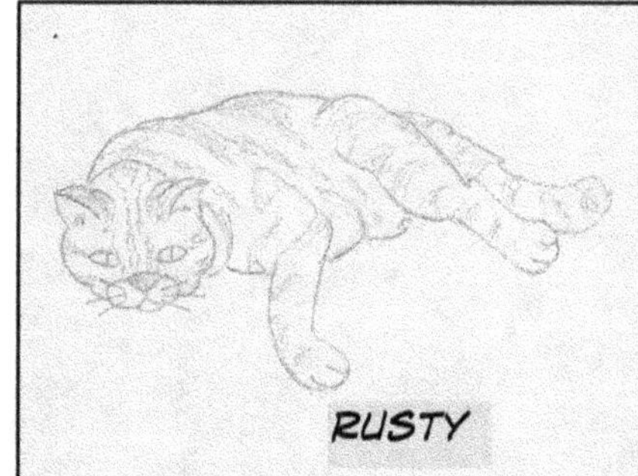

RUSTY

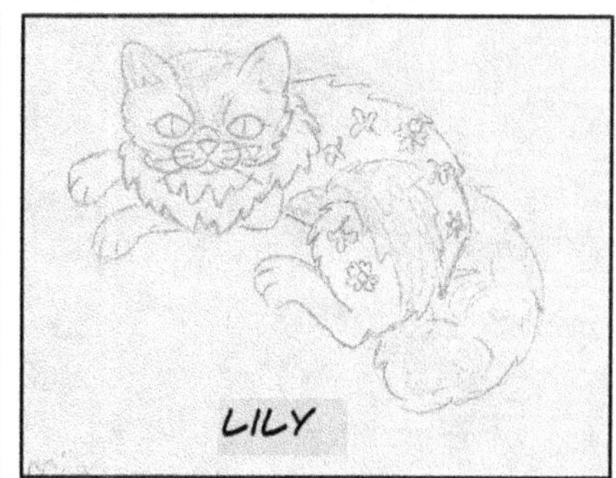

LILY

VOLUME 3 CAST